£14-99

the tao of intimacy and ecstasy

Sounds True
Boulder, CO 80306

© 2014 Solala Towler

SOUNDS TRUE is a trademark of Sounds True, Inc.

The information contained in this book is intended to be educational. Please consult with a qualified medical advisor before practicing the exercises described in this book if you have any health concerns or conditions.

Cover design by Jennifer Miles
Book design by Beth Skelley

Printed in the United States of America

Library of Congress Cataloging-in-Publication Data
Towler, Solala.
  The Tao of intimacy and ecstasy : realizing the promise of spiritual union / Solala Towler.
    pages cm
  ISBN 978-1-62203-196-2
  1. Intimacy (Psychology) 2. Ecstasy. 3. Tao. I. Title.
  BF575.I5T69 2014
  299.5'1444—dc23
                              2013049963

Ebook ISBN 978-1-62203-221-1

10 9 8 7 6 5 4 3 2 1

For Shanti,
the great love of my middle years.

contents

introduction

RELATIONSHIP CAN BE a place of healing, of happiness, and of deep love connection, or it can make us feel lost, alone, and hopeless. It can raise us to the highest levels of radiant beauty, or it can crash us down on the rocks of despair. It can be a place of solace and comfort and instill a deep feeling of belonging, or it can make us sad and bitter and afraid to reach out again.

At the present time, books on relationship are all around us. The bookshelves are full of self-help books on all aspects of relationship—from sex manuals to guidance on creating and sustaining healthy relationships. There are books on spiritual relationship from the viewpoint of various religions and psychotherapies as well as advice books by famous celebrities.

What makes *The Tao of Intimacy and Ecstasy* different from these other books is that it utilizes the unique and ancient wisdom of the Taoist (Daoist) masters from thousands of years of Chinese history to educate, enlighten, and illuminate us so that we may better traverse the challenging and oftentimes shaky ground of sacred union. By *sacred union,* I mean a union that exists on many levels—from day-to-day emotions to heights of sublime ecstasy. A sacred union is a relationship in which both parties have their hearts and eyes wide open. A sacred union is one that allows each partner the space to grow and develop and delve deeply into their own inner landscape while also having a safe place to explore together. A sacred union is a place where wounds—emotional, sexual, physical, or energetic—can have a place and time to heal.

Being in sacred union with another means meeting them on a level playing field, where each person has the right to be heard and seen, not just for who they are when they are at their best, but also for who they are in any present moment. Sacred union encourages each partner to be as open and honest as it is possible in any moment to be, both with

- use sexual energy not only for fun and sensual lovemaking but also as a tool for spiritual cultivation and health enhancement;
- bring your energetic system into balance;
- strengthen your connection to the earth.

Instead of treating sex as merely a physical release, you will be able to bring both a high level of spirituality and a greater depth of pleasure for both you and your partner through the principles and practices of Taoist sexual yoga. Instead of feeling low energy or having multiple health problems, which get in the way of enjoying your life together, you will be able to enjoy greater health and wellbeing through the practice of chi gong. Instead of feeling confused and unclear in your thought processes and emotions, you will be able to attain greater clarity and a stronger emotional balance through both the practices of chi gong and Taoist meditation.

It is often when we are in relationship with others that we can learn to know ourselves in a deeper and richer way. It is my hope that you will be able to take this book and use it in your relationship life to get to know both your partner and yourself in deeper and more profound ways.

Author's Note: All quotations from the *Tao Te Ching* by Lao Tzu and *Inner Chapters* by Chuang Tzu are my own interpretation of the works by these ancient sages. Since I did not translate directly from classical Chinese, I cannot claim that they are translations. I like to call them my "interpretations," as they are the fruit of many years of studying both the texts themselves and the philosophy and practices they teach.

Chapter references are listed after quotes from the *Tao Te Ching* and *Inner Chapters*. Both of these books have had a profound influence on Chinese culture as a whole and especially on Taoism and have remained in print for thousands of years. Many readers find chapter references handy when navigating the different published versions of these texts.

what is taoism?

The Tao is an empty vessel;
it is used but never exhausted.
It is the fathomless source
of the ten thousand beings!

LAO TZU, *TAO TE CHING (CHAPTER 4)*

What Is Tao?

"The Tao that can be told or described in words is not the eternal Tao." So begins the *Tao Te Ching* of Lao Tzu, written some twenty-five hundred years ago. This book has become the most widely translated book in the world after the Bible. It contains much wisdom in its few pages. Lao Tzu's writing is spare and poetic and leaves much room for reflection and meditation.

In addition to being the most well-known book on Tao, it is still studied and chanted each morning in Taoists temples all over China. Lao Tzu was a scholar and spiritual teacher in ancient China, during the Zhou Dynasty (1046–256 BC). Society in that time was falling apart, with each state making war on the other. Civilization, as the ancient Chinese knew it, was crumbling. Despite holding an important and well-paid position in the royal archives, Lao Tzu thought it was time to leave. He headed out to the wild west of China, riding a water buffalo. When he reached the farthest edge of the kingdom, he met up with the person in charge of the garrison there, Yin He, who begged him to write down something of his teachings, so students of Tao would have something to refer to. The legend says that Lao Tzu spent one night there, writing eighty-one short, simple chapters. The next morning he struck out into the wilderness, never to be seen again.

The term *Tao* is used to describe the indescribable, to put into words what is wordless, to give sound to the great silence. Tao can only be pointed to, or referred to, say the ancient sages. It cannot be held, only experienced. It cannot be touched, only felt. It cannot be seen, only glimpsed, with the inner eye. Yet Tao is our source, our path, our end as it is our beginning.

The Chinese word *Tao* is made up of two characters. One means "to follow or to run," and the other means "a human face." Together, these characters can be translated as "a person moving along a path." Tao can also be thought of as the path, or way, itself. Hence, Tao is often referred to as "the Way."

Lao Tzu says:

> You look at it and it is not seen,
> it is called the Formless.
> You listen to it and it is not heard,
> it is called the Soundless.
> You grasp it and it cannot be held,
> it is called the Intangible.
> *(Chapter 14)*

Tao is at once the universal pageant of the constellations and the budding of each new leaf in the spring. It is the constant round of life and death and all that falls between, an undying cycle of change and renewal. While Tao is not personalized, it sustains all of creation, giving life and supporting all living beings—human, plant, animal, water, even the very rock foundation of the earth itself. And, in the end, when we have shrugged off this mortal coil, we return to the bosom of undifferentiated consciousness, Tao.

Followers of the Path of Tao are dedicated to discovering the dance of the cosmos in the passing of each season as well as the passing of each precious moment in our lives. By paying attention only to what we can see with our eyes, we will miss seeing what is really there. It is only by seeing with the inner eye that we can see the true Way. By connecting to our eternal self, by finding a way back to our source, we can experience a sense of peace, of safety, and of harmony with the world around and within us.

The Path of Tao, with its emphasis on self-cultivation and self-responsibility and its many forms of energy work and exercise, is perfect for today's world.

Tao is easy to lose, hard to find, impossible to describe, difficult to see, yet is ever before us, shining like a light in the darkness. Lao Tzu says:

> My words are easy to understand and to apply,
> yet no one understands them
> or puts them into practice.
> *(Chapter 70)*

The Path of Tao

Once there lived men and women who were not conscious of their separation from Tao; therefore, they were at one with it. Chuang Tzu, one of the most important Taoist sages of ancient times, describes this kind of person like this:

> They did not mind being poor. They took no pride in their
> achievements. They made no plans. In this way, they could
> commit an error and not regret it. They could succeed without
> being proud. They could climb mountains without fear, enter
> water without getting wet, and pass through fire without being
> burned. They slept without dreaming and awoke without
> anxiety. Their food was simple and their breath was deep.

3

They did not love life or hate death. When they were born
they felt no elation, when they died there was no sorrow.
Carefree they came. Carefree they went. That was all. They
did not forget their beginning yet did not seek their end.
They accepted all that was given them with delight and when
it was gone, they gave it no more thought. *(Chapter 2)*

Nowadays we strive and struggle, never content, always sure there is
something greater to achieve, something of greater value to attain, if
only we can become successful in the eyes of the world. Yet at the end
of the day, in the deep of the night, or in the first glare of the morning
light, we feel empty and bereft. We have lost the Way and are very far
indeed from those ancient men and woman who lived so lightly and
so well.

It is in acknowledging the interconnectedness of all life that we can
open ourselves to experiencing life in all its manifestations. By paying
close attention to the flow of life around us, we can feel ourselves
being carried along on the currents of energy and spirit that make up
the universe.

The Path of Tao gives us ways to cultivate ourselves spiritually, energetically, and emotionally. It gives us specific practices to bring all our
varying and vying selves into focus, harmony, and the oneness where
we truly dwell—the eternal, ever-evolving Tao.

Tao, then, is the Way—as in direction, as in manner, source, des-
tination, purpose, and process. In discovering and exploring Tao, the
process and the outcome are one and the same. The Way to the goal,
the Way along the way, the one who is going along the Way—they are
all one and the same. Those who think that they can separate out what
is spiritual from what is not spiritual, what is real from what is not real,
what is eternal from what is not eternal—they are lost and confused.
There is no way out or through but through the Way, or Tao, itself. But
just as there are many different kinds of trees in the forest, so too are
there many different approaches to Tao.

All paths are aspects of the one path; all truths are but the one truth. Everything that rises must converge. The men and women of Tao understand this and act accordingly. For them, the past, the present, and the future are of all of a piece. They make no distinctions between things, persons, or states of being. In this way, they free themselves from the cycle of change and dwell in the infinite Tao.

It has been said that words can actually get in the way of true communication. It is when we leave the world of words behind and enter deeply into the world of spirit that we can truly be said to be saying something.

How then are we to be able to "know Tao"? How can we experience, consciously, our connection with the divine? For without the connection to that eternal part of ourselves, all our suffering is in vain. This has been the mystic quest for thousands of years, in many different cultures.

We come from the eternal—before birth—clear and whole. We are then immersed in the dust of the world and lose our clarity, our wholeness. It is only through spiritual work that we can regain that original pure nature, so that at death we can go back into the eternal realm with clear vision and pure understanding. What is good and true about our natures must be cultivated.

Thus, on the Path of Tao, we call spiritual work self-cultivation. We plant the spiritual seeds into our beings and wait patiently for them to grow. We attend them and water them with our tears of joy and grief and mulch them with the negative experiences of our life. And then, if we are patient enough, we can experience the flowering of our Tao nature and flourish like a great flower in the sun.

The Taoist seeks to dig deep beneath all the layers of cultural and psychological silt that has accumulated in us humans over the millennia and to bring forth the shining pearl that lies there.

To enter the Path of Tao means simply to be the best, the most sincere, the most devout, the most understanding, the most patient, the most conscious person we can be. And as such, we can truly call ourselves followers of the grand and divine Way.

the yin/yang symbol

There is rarely a person or situation that is completely yang or completely yin. It is almost always a combination of the two. As we will see later in this book, when we talk about the tai chi of communication, there is often room for both yin and yang energies in any one relationship situation.

One way of understanding this relationship between yin and yang is to use a metaphor from nature, always the preferred way in Taoism. Picture a seed, deep within the darkness of the yin earth, still and waiting there for its birth. There is so much inherent energy in this seed, but without the help of the warm sunlight it will come to nothing. Then, with the proper balance of moisture and sunlight, the little seed germinates and begins to push itself up through the earth toward the light. This growth is its yang aspect. Finally it pushes itself up and grows ever taller in the sunlight to become a plant or even a tree. But eventually, the plant or tree becomes old and begins to die, only to be recovered by the earth and to wait (yin) again for rebirth. Some plants go through this yin-yang cycle again and again.

We, as humans, are also subject to these same laws of yin/yang, change, and transformation. We too grow and flower in our own time and then die, to be reborn again in another body, another life, perhaps even another world. As we will see in later chapters, a relationship can also be born, come to a full flowering, and then transform or "die back" into something altogether different. Such cyclical changes can sometimes mean an enhancement or transformation of the relationship itself, or they can mean that the relationship is ending, perhaps so that another might be born.

It is important to have a balance of yin and yang in our beings if we are to be healthy and happy. Another thing to understand is just what is meant by balance. Real balance does not mean that yin and yang are exactly equal. The image of the circle lets us know that real balance is a constantly shifting thing. Sometimes the yang is fuller than yin; sometimes the yin is fuller than yang. One partner always having the yang role, or being in charge, will not result in a healthy relationship. There needs to be a give-and-take flow in order for each partner to feel empowered and centered, not only in their own being, but also in the relationship itself.

For true balance to be achieved, we need to be open and ready for change and transformation in each moment. Things are constantly shifting, and we need to keep our sense of groundedness so when the earth shifts under our feet, we can go with it and not collapse. The constant balancing, shifting, and rebalancing that goes on between yin and yang reminds us how one day the world and our place in it seems one way, and the next it seems an altogether different place. If we keep that in mind, then we can more easily ride the changes and not be ridden *by* them.

It is a little like riding a surfboard. To successfully surf the ever-changing ocean, we need to find the point of perfect balance so we can ride the waves in a joyful and exciting way and not fall on our face when the first wave hits us. The Taoist practices of meditation and chi gong can be of great help with maintaining this balance. Later chapters will talk about how to use these wonderful tools to enhance our sense of balance and harmony—emotionally, sexually, and spiritually.

Put another way, yin and yang are like a pair of dancers, constantly moving, flowing, and adjusting, so each one is in perfect balance relative to the other's balance. Sometimes their dance is full of grace and lightness. At other times, their dance is clunky or sluggish, up one moment and down another. The more we practice being patient, observant, and open to the changes and transformations both within our own being and within our relationship, the easier it will be to achieve that wonderful sense of yin and yang dancing gracefully, and we will live life in a manner that the ancient Taoists called "free and easy wandering."

The concepts of change and balance are of extreme importance when we talk about relationships. In any relationship, things change, things shift, things evolve or even devolve. If we are too invested in things remaining the same, we will get knocked over and lose our center, our balance, both energetically and emotionally, every time there is a shift in the ground of our relationship.

It is important that shifts in our relationship do not cause us to lose our own way. At times we may feel lost or out of control or even fearful because of what is happening. If we do not lose our own emotional and energetic center, we will be far better able to deal with what is happening in a way that is infused with love and respect, both for ourselves and for our partner.

Difficult or challenging situations and emotional exchanges allow us to engage either our own yin or yang side. Sometimes it is better to move forward with yang energy, to engage in a forceful or dynamic way, while always being careful not to overwhelm or attack our partner. Other times it might be better to remain in a yin state, quietly remaining strong in our groundedness and perhaps giving way to the other person's emotional energy if that is appropriate. Remember, no one aspect is right for every situation. It is best to recognize and be willing to work with the ever-shifting balance of energy in any situation or moment.

It is often said that without the stabilizing energy of the quiet yin, the fiery aggressive energy of yang would have no place to lift off from. Yin energy has been described as "the power behind the throne." Oftentimes the ostentatious showy type of energy depends on the solid backbone energy in the wings to support it.

Just like in the tai chi or yin/yang symbol, each male has a female side as does each female a male aspect. Yang can also be looked at as the dominant role, and yin as the submissive role. Oftentimes one partner in a relationship takes the dominant or the submissive role at all times. This is not true balance. Instead partners should look to trade off roles at different times. We should practice being a leader at times and a follower at other times.

✤ Yin/Yang Reversal Practice

If you are in a relationship where one person tends to be the dominant or yang energy much of the time, try switching roles for a while. If you are used to deferring many decisions to your partner, try being the one to make the decisions; if you are the one who makes most of the decisions, allow your partner to take over that role for a time. If your partner tends to always be in the dynamic leader position in your relationship, allow yourself to be the leader for a time; if you are used to always taking the lead, let go and follow for a while. You will need your partner's cooperation with this practice, but it will be interesting, both for you and your partner.

In Taoist internal alchemy, the metaphors of the Green Dragon and White Tiger are used for yin and yang. It is in the fusion of these two elements that the inner elixir or healing medicine is created. Other times Taoists use the terms *mercury* and *lead*. Mercury is often thought of as yang, while lead is thought of as yin. It is when these two substances are mixed together in the proper amounts and the proper fashion that true alchemy happens.

Another way of saying this is that when the inner female of the male is united with the inner male of the female, then true magic is possible! Not only that, but even with this attraction of opposites, each side must be "drawn out of hiding," and the two sides gathered together so they can become harmonized. This is true union.

It is impossible to be all things to all people. It is even impossible to be all things to one person. Sometimes opposites can complement each other. Sometimes they attract, and then again, sometimes they can repel. If you choose to be in relationship with someone who is too different from you, you will have a hard time staying happy.

The desire for union is inherent in all of us, though it's not always for union with another human being. Sometimes what we may think we are looking for in another person is actually something we are looking for in the divine. In this instance, there is no way that other person can ever live up to our expectations.

By going deep within ourselves, we can get a sense of what it is that we seek in another. Then again, it is also of great importance to learn how to give ourselves what we need. We cannot always be looking for someone else to complete us. That is too great a burden to put onto anyone and usually ends in frustration.

Remember, you are whole and complete just as you are. Take the time for your own self-cultivation instead of merely looking to someone else for your completion.

One of the primary and fundamental practices for connecting with Tao, as well as your own inner being, is through breath. Most people probably think they know how to breathe, but actually they are poor breathers. They either breathe through their mouth instead of through their nose or they breathe very shallowly, filling only the top part of their lungs. And they often breathe as if they were preparing to fight or to flee, which fills them with stress and anxiety.

Chuang Tzu described sages as "the ones who breathe from their heels." This doesn't mean they actually breathed from their feet, but they breathed from deep down in their chest, filling their lungs up completely and pushing down on their diaphragm. Our diaphragm is a dome-shaped, muscular partition separating the thorax from the abdomen. It plays a major role in breathing, as its contraction increases the volume of the thorax and so inflates the lungs. It also has a massaging effect on the organs under it (mainly digestive organs), bringing more blood, lymph, and chi to those organs.

By learning how to breathe more deeply and slowly, we can calm our whole nervous system and allow our digestive system to function more fully.

❧ Taoist Breathing Exercise

Sit on a cushion on the floor or lie on a bed or mat. Through your nose, breathe in very slowly and deeply. Imagine that you are breathing straight into your lower abdomen. In Taoism this area is known as the *dan tian* ("field of elixir"). Then, when you exhale, allow your abdomen to contract.

Try to breathe as slowly and deeply as possible, without causing any stress to your system. Spend at least five to ten minutes at first, then longer as you become used to this breathing. Do this exercise several times a day if you can. You will find that the more you practice breathing this way, the more you will begin to breathe like this all the time, even when you are asleep.

This slow, deep diaphragmatic breathing will bring you a deep sense of peace and harmony. After a while, it will seem as though you are not even breathing at all but are, as my old Zen teacher used to say, "being breathed."

In order to retain the flexibility that Lao Tzu talks about, we have to sustain the quality of *movement* in our lives. This doesn't mean running around madly from one scene to another, one relationship to another, one religion to another, but rather something internal, an openness to change and new experience. Movement implies a dynamic *engagement* with life. And we cannot wait until someone comes along to move us, to complete us, to give our lives form and substance. Moving is something that we ourselves need to do for ourselves. Then, when someone does come along, they will find a whole, harmonized being waiting for them!

It is also important to remember that, to the Taoists, everyone in the universe exists in relationship with everything else. Even for the solitary type, there can be found a solace and a satisfaction in realizing and experiencing, on a root level, this inherent relationship between all life forms. No man or woman is an island indeed!

Lao Tzu says:

> Under heaven everyone knows that the existence of beauty
> depends on the existence of ugliness.
> Everyone knows the capacity of kindness
> depends on the existence of the unkind.
> Existence and nothingness are mutually born,
> difficult and easy complete each other,
> long and short shape each other,
> tall and short rest upon each other,
> sound and music harmonize each other,
> before and after follow one another.
> *(Chapter 2)*

Instead of seeing yin and yang as being at war with one another, we can experience their interaction as a dynamic concert of different yet harmonious notes. This vision of unity and joyful diversity can empower us to live a life of harmonious and exciting engagement.

Finding the Harmony Within

It is very difficult to create harmony with a partner if we are not in harmony within our own self. How we feel about ourselves—physically, emotionally, spiritually, even financially—will have an effect on how others see us and, sometimes, even how we see and experience others.

Poor self-image, a low sense of self-worth, self-destructive habits—all of these will bear on our relationships with others. If we are seeking a love partner—someone who will see us for who we really are, in our best and highest sense—then we need to begin with our own self-cultivation. It's not that we need to be perfect in order to attract someone, but we need to be doing our own work, taking responsibility for our own emotions, and not seeking someone out of desperation. Desperation is not an attractive quality in anyone, especially not someone who is seeking sacred union.

So how do we find that sense of inner harmony within ourselves? Taoism offers many practices for this. Stillness practice, or meditation, is one. Chi gong, or moving meditation, is another excellent way to attain greater harmony, both within and without. (See chapter 13.)

By coming into harmony within ourselves, we are better able to extend that sense of harmony and balance to another. After all, how can we hope to have a harmonious relationship with another if we do not already have that kind of relationship with ourselves?

⁂ Chi Gong Harmony Meditation

Here's a little chi gong meditation practice that you might find helpful for cultivating harmony within.

Sit quietly with eyes closed, breathing from the belly. Inhale, with your abdomen expanding, and say silently to yourself, "I am." Hold the breath for one count and say "at." Then, on your exhale, say "peace." Really feel that this is true. Don't just mouth empty platitudes (even silently).

Practice this "I am at peace" breath nine times or a multiple of nine, such as thirty-six times. You can also say other phrases, such as "I am in harmony" or "I am healing." Or you can practice with your partner and use the phrase "We are at peace" or "We are in harmony."

The combination of breath work and silent mantra will stabilize this harmonious feeling. This meditation is so simple you can do it at any time, but be sure to go slowly and really feel it.

ᘓᕀ Swallowing Yang Essence

Stand or sit facing the sun, eyes closed. With your mind intent, inhale yang energy from the sun down into your lower abdomen, three to nine times or even thirty-six times. Feel this energy heating up your lower dan tian and then circulating throughout your body. This is a good practice for someone who is feeling a lack of yang energy manifesting as low overall energy or low sexual energy.

When we find ourselves often becoming angry or fearful or overly critical of others, it means that we have lost our own center. Taoists have a term for someone who is in touch with their essential or authentic self: *tzu ran*. We see this term a lot in the *Tao Te Ching* and the *Chuang Tzu*, and scholars often mistranslate it as "the perfect man." The Chinese term actually is better translated as "authentic or realized person."

This is the kind of person who is in touch with their natural, essential self. They do not seek to find meaning for themselves in someone else. They do not look for completion of themselves in someone else. They do not seek their own balance in someone else but instead look for it within themselves.

How are we to achieve this state of being? According to traditional Taoist thought, truly wise people are not aware of their wisdom; therefore, they are wise. A truly foolish person tries to be wise and therefore is not. The sage dwells on what is profound and deep and not on what is only on the surface. They dwell in the eternal and not on what is transient. They prefer the fruit over the flower.

Lao Tzu tells us:

> Heaven is eternal.
> Earth is eternal.
> The reason they are eternal
> is because they do not live for themselves.
> This is why they are eternal.
> The sage places himself to the rear
> yet always ends up at the front.
> He is not concerned with his own safety
> yet he always remains safe.
> Is it not because he is selfless
> that he is able to realize his true self?
> *(Chapter 7)*

Most of us are not sages or enlightened beings, but that need not stop us from having enlightened attitudes and attempting to put those attitudes into practice. The question is, are we that superior person who is ready to let down our defenses, let go of our fears and doubts, and begin the long and often difficult and challenging quest to discover who we really are?

To become a sage, to become a wise man or woman, takes a level of commitment not found in the ordinary person. It is not something you can learn in a weekend workshop or from reading a book (even this one) or by watching a video. Teachers can certainly be helpful, but it is really one's own self-cultivation that will produce the light to illuminate your life and help you to realize your own essential nature.

Here's how Chuang Tzu described such people:

> The ancient sages were not attached to life nor did they fear
> death. To them, being born was nothing special, nor was
> death. Carefree they came into this world and carefree they
> went out of it. They did not worry too much about where

they came from, nor did they worry about where they were going. They accepted whatever they were given with joy and gratitude but often gave it away in turn. They did not use their mind to resist the Tao and did not try to divine the ways of heaven. This is what I call the true sage. With this kind of person—their mind is free, their spirit is calm, and their brow is smooth. *(Chapter 2)*

Many people rush around trying to find happiness. They often pursue it with a grim determination. Many times they may find themselves on the verge of happiness only to have it stolen away from them, or so they feel. They keep looking for happiness in either outward riches or in another person. In their grim determination, they are actually pushing happiness away from them. The Taoist view is that we cannot find happiness until we stop looking for it.

On the other hand, we all have desires. We may have a desire to be a better person, to progress on the spiritual path, to become a better lover, better friend, and better partner. These desires are what lead us to learn just how to do that. So the desires themselves are not necessarily a problem; it is how we act on them and how controlled we are by them that can be a problem.

Again, if we are not in harmony with ourselves, how can we expect to be in harmony with someone else? If we do not feel whole and unfragmented within ourselves, how can we expect to feel that way with someone else? If we do not feel at home in our own body, how can we feel at home with someone else's body? If we are not familiar with our own energy currents and cycles, how can we align ourselves with someone else's energy? If we are controlled by our emotions, how can we expect to be in harmony with someone else's emotions? If we are unhealthy and depressed, how can we offer something worthwhile to someone else?

The answer is that we cannot. This does not mean that we need to be perfect and have our act totally together before we can approach someone else. It means that we need to at least be aware of our problems and be willingly and actively working on them before we can expect to reach a level of sacred union with another. If you are the type of person who finds it very hard to ever admit to being wrong or if you are in a relationship with someone like this, it can be very difficult, if not downright impossible, to reach the higher levels of relationship. (See chapter 12.)

❧ Swallowing Yin Essence

Stand or sit facing the moon, eyes open or closed.
Inhale the yin energy of the moon into your lower
dan tian, in your lower abdomen, three to nine times,
or up to thirty-six times. Feel the cool watery energy
of the moon enter you, balancing all the hot centers
of your body. Do this practice if you feel you have
too much yang energy, which manifests as feelings of
anxiety or overstimulation, too many thoughts going
on in your head, and insomnia.

We all have problems and possibilities. We all have things that need polishing. We are all living in the material world, with all its inherent problems. Yet at the same time, we are all divine beings, and as such, we are all capable of doing divine work and being in sacred union with ourselves, our partner, and our spiritual source, whether we call it Tao or God or the Great Mystery.

It is in learning how to live in harmony—with our surroundings, our job, our health issues, our friends and community, and our divine partner—that we will be able to achieve a deep level of relationship I call sacred union.

the tao of sex
and relationship

Of all things that make man prosper, none can be compared to sexual intercourse. It is modeled after Heaven and takes its pattern by Earth; it regulates Yin and rules Yang. Those who understand its significance can nurture their nature and prolong their years; those who miss its true meaning will harm themselves and die before their time.

MASTER TUNG HSUAN

THE ANCIENT TAOIST view of sex is extremely different from modern attitudes about this most primal of human expressions. Taoism teaches us how to use this primal urge to facilitate greater communication and trust levels with our partners. Taoism is concerned with the basic male-female attraction and interaction, as well as the ability to use our own individual sexual energy to further ourselves in our quest for better health (physical, emotional, and psychological) and a greater sense of spirituality. Taoists are eminently practical. They developed a way to use sex as a tool and a practice for communication, communion, self-awareness, energy exchange, and personal health, all at the same time!

Like Taoist philosophy itself, Taoist sexual yoga is governed by cycles and seasons, by an awareness of our own energetic system as well as that of our partner. Its attitudes and practices are ways to tap into our energy and not only share it with our partner but also direct it within ourselves. It casts no moral judgments upon the sexual act itself and would laugh good naturedly at anyone who tried to do so. Instead, it offers healthy and productive ways of being sexual, both within our bodies and with those we love.

The Art of the Bedchamber

The teachings known as "the Art of the Bedchamber" originate with Huangti, the Yellow Emperor, that ancient, perhaps mythical, sage-king. The teachings themselves are believed to have been taught to him by three immortal maidens, who came to him one evening when he was burdened by the heavy weight of royal responsibility to his concubines. Because he was the symbol of the health and welfare of the entire kingdom, his ability to cohabitate with his vast assemblage of concubines and wives was a symbol of the vitality of the kingdom as a whole. With literally hundreds and sometimes thousands of women to satisfy, it was no wonder that the king found himself becoming extremely worn out! Fortunately for him, and fortunately for the men of today, there is a way to not only satisfy both his partner and himself, but also to retain his vital energy in the process. This is what the three immortal maidens taught Huangti so long ago.

Picture a dispirited and distraught emperor pacing in his quarters, when suddenly three maidens appear before his tired eyes. They are clearly from another world. They bow gracefully and ask about the welfare of the sovereign.

"I am exhausted and in disharmony," Huangti says to his illustrious visitors. "I am sad and worry constantly." He looks at them with hollow eyes. "I fear that I am not up to the task of emperor if I cannot perform my duties as the royal husband," he says, wringing his hands. "What shall I do about this?"

One of the maidens, Su Nu, or "the Plain Girl," says that all his problems can be attributed to faulty ways of loving. "Women," she says, "are stronger in sex, and men who do not know the true Way of loving will die before their time. Not only that, but they will die without enjoying the pleasure of living."

At first Huangti is not convinced. Those long nights with his multiple wives have been wearing him out! "I cannot think that I will ever make love again," he says.

"No," the maidens tell him, "that is the wrong attitude." They then tell how yin and yang have their activities and changes and that humans must not do anything against the course of nature (wu wei).

"Yin and yang must be in clear communication, or they will not be able to harmonize with each other," they say.

"How then," he asks of his illustrious visitors, "can I continue to have relations with so many woman and not exhaust myself but be in harmony with them?"

The three maidens tell him how to make love and control his emissions. The latter is very beneficial to man's health. At this, the emperor perks up and so spends the next several nights in close communion with his three immortal teachers, learning further practices and ideas on the proper way to make love in tune with the Tao. Thus, the Art of the Bedchamber was born.

At the very heart of the Art of the Bedchamber, or the Tao of Sex, is the notion that woman is both energetically and sexually superior to man. Woman is considered to be the repository of inexhaustible yin, while man is caught up in his all-too-quickly exhaustible yang. Applying this belief to other aspects of life, it also means women are more often capable of sustained efforts and are more conscious of long-term goals and effects.

Men, unconsciously acknowledging the superiority of women in this way, have feared and envied them and, consciously and unconsciously, used this fear and envy as a tool of oppression for thousands of years. This explains much of the history of "mankind" over the last several millennia.

Taoists venerate the yin, the valley spirit, the primordial woman, unlike most modern religions, which were founded by and are presided over by men who maintain that the creator and sustainer of the universe is male. This has left little room for the female, other than to be the mother, virgin, and bride.

Lao Tzu tells us:

> Know the strength of the masculine
> but preserve the feminine.
> Remaining receptive to all under heaven,
> do not separate yourself from the eternal virtue *(te)*.
> Become again as a child.
> Know the white (yang) but hold to the black (yin).
> Serve as a model for all under heaven.
> Serving as a model for all under heaven
> and not deviating from the eternal virtue,
> one returns to the primordial origin *(wuji)*.
> *(Chapter 28)*

The Tao of Sex is a way of acknowledging the energetic superiority of the woman while training the man to be able to meet her on equal and solid ground to their mutual benefit. Once men and women can meet on a level playing field, the age-old conflict between the sexes will become a thing of the past.

Sexual Energy and Essence

Woman, being yin, or water, is slow to warm—in contrast to the male, who is yang, or fire, and who flares up immediately. The danger is that, in his sudden flaring, he will continue past the woman and leave her far behind, just as she is coming to a boil. If a man climbs onto the woman with limited foreplay, bangs away at her until he reaches orgasm, and then is done, the woman will feel frustrated and unfulfilled. Over time, those feelings will affect her emotionally as well as energetically, causing her to feel more frustrated and often angry as well. Her anger and frustration will manifest in all sorts of ways that, on the surface, seem to have nothing to do with sex but still cause problems between her and her partner.

Taoist sex offers us a different scenario: the man matches his energy level to the woman's, and they come to a slow or quick boil together. Instead of sex being a rapid climb up the mountain, with orgasm (especially the male's, but also the female's) as the peak goal, lovemaking becomes a goalless and joyful event, a marvelous dance between two people who are enjoying each other and themselves. It becomes more of a long, even sharing and less of a sudden peaking with an equally sudden drop.

In the Tao of Sex there is not only an emotional and physical exchange but also an equally important and vital exchange of energy through the exchange of bodily fluids. When a man ejaculates into his woman partner, she can absorb his precious fluid through the extremely porous membranes of her vagina. Thus, he gives her an infusion of nourishing yang essence, which she then combines with her own innate yin to bring herself into a more harmonious balance. When a woman has an orgasm, she too generates her own precious substance, which the man can absorb through his own organ, also very porous, especially at the head. In this way, he receives an infusion of her precious yin essence, which he then combines with his own innate yang in order to bring himself into an equally harmonious balance.

However, as the tale of the Yellow Emperor tells us, ejaculation significantly depletes a man's energy. Most of us are familiar with the post-lovemaking scenario in which the woman wants to sit up and talk and cuddle and perhaps continue with more lovemaking, while the man, utterly exhausted and used up, rolls over and goes to sleep, leaving the woman frustrated, lonely, and often angry. The man seems like an unfeeling, uncaring oaf, concerned only with his own pleasure and all too ready to drop out as soon as that pleasure is experienced. The seemingly oafish behavior is a result of his body's reaction to what has just happened. Most men are all too familiar with the sudden, empty feeling that happens immediately after ejaculation. The woman who was so desirable and exciting minutes ago is suddenly almost too much to bear. We would like to just lie back and take it easy or perhaps take a short nap. Meanwhile she is still ready to go on to new exciting heights, making us feel deficient and irritated. We have been taught that these feelings are normal. We have become used to the idea that once we have attained orgasm, we are no longer interested in sex.

One moment we feel juicy and electric and powerful. The next we feel like a deflated balloon. And what's just as bad, if not worse, is that that wonderful juicy, electric, powerful feeling only lasted a few minutes. It seems as though, just when we thought we were getting a handle on it, it slipped out from under us and left us washed up on the shore like a beached whale! This is not the way we would like to feel after a wonderful lovemaking session.

In order to understand why a man's body reacts this way to orgasm, we need to know just what is involved in ejaculation and what it is that is ejaculated. Semen itself contains vitamins, minerals, hormones, and proteins, among other things. This precious fluid is made up of nutrients taken from all parts of the body and is composed of a large amount of cerebrospinal fluid.

Many of the ancient Taoists equated losing semen, or *jing,* with losing the essence of life itself. Jing is one of "the Three Treasures"—jing, chi, and *shen*—three essential life energies. Jing is said to reside in the kidneys and rules sexual and creative energy, as well as the body's constitution. In Chinese medicine, birth defects are considered a problem with jing.

Jing also rules the aging process. We are all born with a finite amount of jing. Some of us are born with strong jing. These are the kind of people who can abuse themselves for a long time before they have to pay for it. They also tend to be athletic and have a strong constitution. Others are born with weaker jing and have to pay more attention to their diet, exercise, and other aspects of health in order to lead healthy lives. No matter how much jing we have, as we grow older, this jing is used up, and we experience the typical signs of the aging process—hair loss, dry skin, weakened bones, lower vitality. Even though jing cannot be replaced, it can be supported and made stronger by maintaining a healthy lifestyle and by energetic practices such as chi gong and tai chi.

Since women do not lose jing in the same way as men, they tend to live a lot longer. Women do lose jing during childbirth and at menses, but since they stop menstruating and having children as they age, their chi depletion decreases accordingly. This is one reason, in the Taoist view, women live longer than men. Just visit a retirement home some time and see the huge difference in population with women far outnumbering men!

If a man squanders his jing in an unhealthy lifestyle or from too much unhealthy sex, his aging process is sped up, and he ages and dies much faster. If he practices the Tao of Sex, any man can have more energy and a stronger constitution and live a longer and richer life. And, as sexual energy is also what fuels the brain, his mind will be clearer and more flexible as well.

While it can deplete a man each time he gives up his precious substance, it does not deplete the woman to give up hers. She is able to give her essence generously without loss to herself. So in Taoist sex, a man is encouraged to bring the woman to complete fulfillment as often as he can, while controlling himself in the process. In this way, he will conserve his own precious essence while absorbing hers.

If this doesn't seem quite fair to the woman, who is giving up her essence without receiving his, remember that energetically the woman is far stronger than the man, and an occasional infusion of yang is usually sufficient to keep her happy and healthy. In the meantime, she has her man working most diligently to make sure she reaches fulfillment as often as possible!

The Optional Orgasm

What is that mysterious art that allows a man to master his sexual energy, for his own health, for the satisfaction of his partner, and for more intimate, more satisfactory lovemaking? Primarily, it is the art of ejaculation control or *optional ejaculation.*

At first, the idea of giving up the orgasm is very difficult, if not downright impossible, for most men to accept. After all, isn't that what sex is all about? Sex without the release of orgasm might seem like a joyless and uninteresting affair at first, but the new levels of experience it opens up can quickly make it just as exciting, if not more so, than the old way of lovemaking.

Sex without the goal of orgasm takes a little practice and a lot of trust, self-discipline (as opposed to self-denial), and surrender. The key word here is *surrender.* It is in the act of surrendering to his partner and to the discipline of lovemaking without ejaculation that the man has the chance to surrender to Tao itself. For a man to surrender, both to his partner and to the moment they are sharing, may be a challenge, but when he does, that precious moment is expanded and carried over into the rest of his and his partner's lives. When he surrenders—to the moment of sharing, the moment of yielding, the moment of physical and psychic attunement with his partner as well as within himself—the man has the opportunity to expand both within and without to the greater moment, the greater union, the greater attunement, to what we call Tao.

This surrender applies to the woman as well. She too is able to relax, to forget about performing, about pleasing her partner at a cost to herself. She too is able to let go and feel her own energy move within her body and then out and into her partner's.

It is only through a prolonged and emotionally bonded relationship that this kind of optional-ejaculation practice can succeed. It is crucial for a man to work with a partner who supports him in this practice. Otherwise it will be too easy for the woman to push him over the edge. She too must be willing to open to this practice herself if her partner is ever going to succeed.

Occasionally she may decide to give up her own orgasm. Some Taoist teachers say women should control their need to have orgasms.

While orgasm is not actually as physiologically harmful for the woman as it is for the man, if they want to truly meet on the same level, she also needs to give a little in this department. In this way, both partners may experience the joy of lovemaking as a goalless act.

In this way, lovemaking can become a two-way experience, in which both partners are able to give to as well as receive from each other. Sometimes lovemaking culminates in the release of orgasm in one or both partners, sometimes not. What people find in this style of love-making is that the need for the physical release of orgasm becomes less of a pressure and more of an option. Together they form a double helix as their combined energies spiral into and out of each other.

How to Control Ejaculation

Just how is optional ejaculation accomplished? Like all Taoist practices, it is quite simple but takes sensitivity and a little practice.

To begin with, the man pays close attention to when he is reaching "the point of no return," or when he is close to ejaculation. Then he stops thrusting and, keeping himself still within his partner, breathes deeply and slowly until he feels ready to resume thrusting again. The key is for him to be able to be sensitive enough to his body to be able to tell when he is reaching that point without going past it.

It is often helpful to constrict the anus and pull up on the testicles. Holding the breath for a moment or so, until the urge to ejaculate is over, is also helpful.

Another option is to put pressure on the urethra (the tube through which the semen travels) itself by pressing the point halfway between the anus and the scrotum. In Chinese medicine, this point is known as Conception Vessel 1, as it is the first of several points along the Conception Vessel meridian; in common sexual parlance, it is sometimes called "the million dollar point." By pressing with two or three fingers directly on this point just prior to ejaculation, the man can cause the semen to remain within the body instead of being lost outside of his body. At the very least, this practice will cut down measurably on the amount of semen ejaculated and, therefore, the amount of energy lost. Eventually, after much practice in sensitivity and mind and breath control, a man will be able to stop ejaculation without manual intervention.

By the way, I would not recommend using controlled ejaculation as a form of birth control until you have mastered it completely.

How Often?

How often a man may safely ejaculate depends on a variety of factors such as his age, his level of general health, and even the time of year. For instance, in the summer, when the air is warm or hot, a man may ejaculate much more often than in the winter, when he needs more vital energy to keep his body warm. Also, if his health is good, he will not suffer the loss of energy as much as he would if he were in poor health or a weak state due to injury or medical intervention.

Sun S'su Mo, a very famous physician who was born in 581 CE and lived to be 101 years old, offered this formula: a man of twenty can have an emission every four days; a man of thirty, every eight days; a man of forty, every ten days; a man of fifty, every twenty days; and a man of sixty, once a month.

The ancient Chinese also offered several admonitions about when not to engage in sex. It was taught that in times of great seismic or meteorological disturbance, the chi, or electromagnetic energy, in the air can be very disturbing to our own personal chi, or energy system, so making love during these times is not conducive to good energetic control and sharing. There was also an injunction against making love while intoxicated or under extreme emotional conditions. It would be very difficult to remain sufficiently sensitive, both to one's self and to one's partner at such a time.

There is leeway for each individual to find his own rate of emission. Experiment and find out for yourself what works for you. Taking into account the season, your age, and your current health status, you will be able to experiment and find out for yourself what works and doesn't work. Taoists should never submit to rigid, dogmatic codes of any sort but explore within reasonable boundaries in order to find out just what is right for their personal cultivation.

Once you have had some experience with Taoist sexual practices, you may find that when you do ejaculate, it is often much stronger and much more of a whole-body orgasm. You can feel energy rushing through your whole body in a powerful yet pleasant way. You may jerk and twitch a bit while this is going on; it is a good idea to let your sexual partner know this may happen (if she doesn't already) so she will not be afraid that you are having some sort of fit!

After a long time of practice, you will also find that when you do ejaculate, you will not lose energy but will even gain energy, especially if there is true communion or energy exchange with your partner.

Don't be daunted by the seeming difficulty of this method of lovemaking. It will take a little while to master, so don't worry or get too frustrated with yourself for "blowing it," especially at the beginning. It may even feel a little awkward and unnatural at first but once you get the hang of it, it will seem extremely natural and simple. The willingness to try something new and the cooperation of your partner (extremely important) will help you on your way to becoming a "seminal kung fu master."

Sensitivity and Slowness

Taoist sexual practices require a high level of sensitivity on both sides. Cultivating one's sensitivity not only heightens the levels of pleasure and response in each partner but also sensitizes each partner to the other. It is not possible to learn Taoist sexual practices without first cultivating this level of sensitivity in both partners.

Controlling ejaculation is difficult if you're not sensitive to what's really happening in your body, and it's difficult to be sensitive when you're going eighty miles an hour. According to the Kinsey Report, three quarters of all men in the United States ejaculate within two minutes or less! Then we're back to the scenario of the slow-to-boil woman being left behind by the quick-to-flame-out man. A slower pace, besides allowing you the space to feel what is going on in your body, slows down the whole lovemaking session, allowing it to go on much longer.

Slowing down also allows you to be sensitive to what is going on in your partner's body. All too often, what happens when a man and woman make love is that, essentially, the man is using the woman to masturbate. The myth of a woman having a climax simply by a man moving inside her is exactly that, a myth. Most women require some sort of external stimulation, either from herself or from her partner. A man can stimulate a woman with his penis, his fingers, or his tongue.

Remember, in Taoist lovemaking it is the job of the man to serve the woman. Some women want a lot of foreplay, some need very little. If you are in doubt about something, don't be afraid to ask. Most women like being able to be open with their lovers about what works for them and what does not. If you are able to be a generous and thoughtful lover, she will open to you all the more deeply. And when a woman opens herself, both physically and emotionally, to a man, then both will reach the heights of sacred union.

Both partners should be sure to take time to discover just what kinds of things give the other pleasure. Don't assume that because one thing worked with the last lover you were with, it will work with your new lover. And don't assume that because one thing worked the last time you were making love to your partner, it will work the next time. Take some time to explore together what works for the two of you. Don't be afraid to try out new things, but also don't let it disturb you if your partner doesn't want something new.

Women's Sexuality

As mentioned, women's sexual energy is quite different from men's. Women are water, slow to boil, unlike men, who are fire, quick to flare up and out. Yet while women are yin, it is not always their role to receive. Oftentimes they are able to express their sexual energy to a male partner in a way that their partner can receive. In other words, it is not necessary to be bound by the conceptual ideas of what is female and what is male. It is the balance point that Taoists seek in order to bring themselves into balance and harmony. Plants need both water (yin) and sunlight (yang) in order to grow and thrive. Too much of one or the other can either dry a plant up or drown it. Both men and women need a balance of yin and yang within their individual selves, and a relationship between two people also needs a balance of yin and yang. Which partner supplies the yin and which supplies the yang can vary throughout the course of the relationship.

In Taoist sexual cultivation, women are not merely receptacles for absorbing male fluids and energy, but are also able to absorb their own fluids and energy to enhance their own health and wellbeing. The powerful energies that are created through lovemaking benefit women on many different levels—sexual, emotional, psychological, and energetic, as well as spiritual, as we shall see in chapter 4.

Because of the way that women are energetically built, they can enjoy almost unlimited sexual pleasure. As noted earlier, during orgasm, instead of their sexual fluids and energy flowing up and out, as men's do, they flow down and in, so there is no energetic loss. However, women can be drained from too much or too intense lovemaking. That movie image of two people crashing into each other to have sex can be very damaging to women. Too forceful penetration can damage the delicate tissues of the vagina. Too deep penetration can even damage the uterus.

It is important for a man not to pressure a woman into having sex if she is not in the mood or energetically up to it. A woman should never be pressured to extend herself and her energy to a man. Asking her to give when she is not willing or able is infantile behavior of a man, and it will not only damage the woman energetically but emotionally as well. Many men live in a state of hyperarousal pretty much all of the time, and though there may be some women who also experience themselves that way, most do not. For a man to force a woman to give herself to him or a woman to force herself to give in to the man when she is not ready usually leads to negative experiences for both the woman and the man. On the other hand, if the man takes the time to allow the woman to truly meet him energetically and emotionally, it will definitely benefit them both.

Many women have not had the experience of a Taoist lover, so they may go through their entire life nonorgasmic and frustrated or even wounded about sex. Many men approach sex in a basically infantile fashion, focused on what they can get from the women and thus putting women into a "mommy" role. The Taoist admonition that the man should serve the woman can change the sexual experience of the woman, shifting her away from being a mommy and into experiencing herself as a goddess, to be adored and brought to complete sexual fulfillment.

While men lose energy with each ejaculation, women only lose it with the blood loss of menstruation or childbirth. For some women the loss of energy during menses can be significant. Practicing chi gong, such as the essence chi gong form at the end of this book, will help considerably with this. Ancient Taoist women developed various chi gong practices to actually stop their menses. This is called Slaying the Red Dragon and involves breast massage and vaginal locks. It is a subject that is beyond the scope of this book, but there is material out there if you wish to pursue this more seriously. (*Healing Love Through the Tao* by Mantak Chia is an excellent source.)

⋓ Deer Exercise

Breast massage can be used for general breast health as well as uterine health, as the breasts and uterus are energetically connected. The Deer Exercise can facilitate breast circulation, help prevent fibroid tumors, and tonify the muscles in both the vagina and anus to help prevent prolapse of the uterus.

Sit cross-legged, with the heel of one foot pressing against your vagina. Rub your hands together at least thirty-six times to warm them up, then gently rub your breasts in a circular motion from inside to outside, avoiding the tender nipple area. Do this at least thirty-six times, once or twice a day.

Now, as you inhale, pull up and tighten the muscles of your vagina and anus. Press the tip of your tongue onto the roof of your mouth and breathe in through the nose. Imagine that you are pulling up energetically from the perineal area to the point in the center of your breasts (the middle dan tian, or heart center) and then from there to the upper dan tian, at the crease between the eyebrows, and into the pituitary gland in the center of your brain. Hold the tension for a moment or so, then exhale and completely relax. (The relaxation is as important as the tension.) You may do this thirty-six times or fewer as well.

Just as a man can postpone his impending orgasm to extend lovemaking, so too can a woman postpone hers to enhance and deepen the orgasm experience. As soon as you feel the orgasm coming, completely relax your mind as well as your body. This may stop or slow down the orgasm. The next time you feel your energy building toward orgasm, completely relax again. Allow the build-up to occur again, and this time allow the orgasm to unfold. It will not be focused entirely on your genitals but will flow in waves throughout your body, which means that instead of your orgasmic energy staying in your genital area, it can travel throughout your body. You can consciously direct this energy upward to your heart center or to your pituitary gland, or you can just relax and let it go where it will. (This technique is particularly helpful for women, but it can also be a great experience for men, who are used to only experiencing the orgasmic pleasure in one small area of their bodies.)

The more both men and woman understand how the fundamental energy of women differs from that of men and how to support, work with, and dance with it, the more the sexual relationship between them will flourish and provide healing and great pleasure to both partners.

A Different View of Sex and Sexuality

Sex is probably the most loaded word in the English language. For many people, it is such an overwhelming and difficult subject that they don't even know where to begin. Sex, or what passes for sex, permeates Western society and is used to sell everything from cars to politics. Sex is talked about and written about and even sung about almost more than any other subject, yet most people still know appallingly little about it. Mostly what people are talking about, writing about, and singing about is the *idea* of sex. And this *idea* has become so complicated and convoluted that hardly anyone has a clue as to what sex is really about.

Some may view sex as a great and tangled mystery full of pitfalls and danger. Others think of sex as exciting, titillating, powerful, or frightening. Sometimes it's regarded as all of these things simultaneously! Unreal images of what is sexy and provocative are fed to us by the media, causing most people to feel they don't measure up. They know deep down inside that they will never achieve the level of perfection and glamour pictured for them by the media, and they feel cheated, angry, depressed, frightened, and powerless.

This *idea* of sex steals people's sense of personal power, self-respect, and self-love. In their anger and despondency over what they perceive to be their own and their partner's sexuality, many people act out in violent or unhealthy ways. The rise of sexual abuse, especially of children, is indicative of that anger. Many people can only feel sexually powerful with someone much smaller or less powerful. In the past, this dynamic has been brought to bear on women, who were seen as "the weaker sex." Not all women are content to be the weaker sex these days, and in their drive to be the equal or stronger sex, conflict between the sexes arises.

So many layers of morality and control and misunderstood emotional garbage are built into the idea of sex that it is no wonder many people have such a hard time with sex. And our society's emphasis on the rush, the high, the peak experience hasn't helped any. Sex has become a commodity, bought and sold just like any other commodity, and is one of the biggest industries in the world, built on greed, abuse, and control.

Taoist sexual practices offer an alternative to this view; one that is healthy and positive. The man serves the woman, giving her primacy over him. There is a continued sharing of energy, trust, intimacy, and pleasure between both partners and emphasis is placed on safe and healthy sexual practices that can build energy rather than tear it down. In today's world of deadly sexually transmitted diseases, it is even more important to practice safe sex than ever before. By safe sex, I am speaking not only of sex that does not spread disease but that also does not drain the body of needed energy and vitality and that is based on mutual love and respect.

Ancient Taoists held a playful and poetic attitude toward sex. The phrase "clouds and rain" was used to describe the sexual act; the clouds refers to the ova of the earth, and rain is the sperm of heaven. Terms such as *jade gate* and *cinnabar cleft* for the vagina, *jade terrace* and *precious pearl* for the clitoris, *inner gate* for the cervix, and *golden valley* for the vulva are all indicative of the Taoists' attitude. Jolan Chang lists eight names for the vagina alone, including *lute string* for the depth of one inch, *water chestnut teeth* for the level of two inches, *inner door* for the level of seven inches, and *north pole* for the level of eight inches! The eight depths together are "the eight valleys."

While there are numberless names for a woman's sexual anatomy, there are only a few, such as *jade stem* and *turtle head,* for the man's special parts. This is in keeping with the deep veneration for women, which plays such a large part in Taoist thought and attitude.

Taoists say that it takes seven years to know the rhythms of a woman's body, seven years to learn her mind, and seven years to understand her spirit. How many men are willing and able to put in this kind of time to truly and deeply understand their partners?

The women's movement of the last forty years or so has made it clear what women want from men and also what they do not want. Women want self-empowerment; a feeling of co-responsibility with their partner, along with accountability; a sense of self-worth that is not based on glamour or how much value they possess in the sexual marketplace; a feeling of mutual trust and intimacy; and the knowledge that they are accepted for whom and what they really are.

This is just what the Tao of Sex is all about. Taoist sexual practices are really not possible without a deep sense of trust and in turn, the intimacy that trust generates. When a man practices the Tao of Sex, he is acknowledging that what he and his partner are doing is worth a little work, a little effort, a small amount of self-control, in order for them both to reach even higher levels of ecstasy, communion, and communication. And the woman is acknowledging that she is willing to support and help him with this achievement, for both their sakes.

Techniques and Positions

While it is important not to get too hung up in physical techniques at the expense of deep soul connection, there are a few simple things that we can do to make the experience of sex more energetically healthy and powerful.

Just going slowly, especially for the man, is probably the most important "technique" of all. Remember, the man is fire while the woman is water. While women may vary in their excitement processes, it is always best to stoke his fire slowly in order to bring her water to a boil, rather than firing up quickly and then going down in flames before the woman has even come to a simmer.

An ancient Taoist text, *The Designated Essentials of the Jade Bedroom*, states: "In general, the way to control woman is first to play and amuse gently, causing the spiritual (qualities) to harmonize and the intent to

42

feel moved. After a good long while (of this), you can have intercourse and insert the jade stalk within."

A famous guidance for the man called "nine shallow, one deep" describes a lovemaking practice of the man entering the woman only in a shallow way, and with just the head of the jade stalk penetrating her nine times. This is followed by one deep thrust. This practice will help the man control himself as well as titillate the woman. There are many other versions of this practice, such as going on to eight shallow thrusts followed by two deep thrusts and on to seven shallow, then three deep, and so on.

Another thing a man can do is pull up the muscles in his anus when he withdraws from the woman and relax them when thrusting in. (He is actually pulling up on the pelvic floor.) Or, if he is close to orgasm, he should just stop thrusting and pull up on his anus. With a little practice, this action will stop the ejaculation from happening. Then he can resume his thrusting while still paying close attention to when he is getting close to ejaculating.

There are also many exercises and massage techniques both the man and woman can use on themselves or their partners that will help with healthy and strong sexual energy. It is very important not to get too bogged down in technical details and lose the heart connection. But a little knowledge can make things healthier and more interesting.

Many sexual positions recommended by the ancient Chinese have fanciful names such as *A Phoenix Plays in a Red Cave, Leaping Wild Horses, Mandarin Ducks Entwined, Reeling Off Silk, Fluttering and Soaring Butterfly,* and *Mystic Bird Soaring Over the Ocean.* Many of them require great flexibility, and some even require the help of a third person (in ancient times usually a maid) to help support one of the participants! The nine basic positions, however, can be done by most reasonably healthy adults.

1. *Dragon Turning Over.* The woman lies on her back, face up, while spreading her thighs open as wide as she can. The

man lies on top of her. He thrusts about five inches into her vagina and moves with leisurely yet powerful strokes. This position is good for toning sexual energy and for deep communion and communication between partners.

2. *Two Tigers.* The woman lies face down with her buttocks up. The man approaches her, on his knees, from behind, inserting his jade stalk into her jade gate as deeply as he can, while refraining from thrusting too forcefully. This position is a good energy builder for both partners and is especially good for the heart and liver of the male (or yang) partner.

3. *Playful Monkeys.* The woman lies on her back with a pillow under her buttocks. She raises her legs so that she can lay them over her partner's shoulders. The man inserts his jade stalk into her jade gate and, moving a little deeper each time, performs the nine shallow, one deep thrusting pattern. When the woman "rejoices" (reaches orgasm), he stops. This position is said to increase hardness of the erection and to lengthen the man's staying power, as well as strengthen his spirit.

4. *Cicadas Mating.* The woman lies on her stomach while the man, leaning gently on her, enters her from behind. As he moves into her, she should raise her buttocks slightly. The woman contracts her vagina as he thrusts into her and allows it to dilate when he retreats. This technique is said to eradicate the "seven illnesses"—anger, depression, sorrow, remorse, fear, selfishness, and nervousness.

5. *Mounting Tortoises.* The woman lies on her back with her knees bent up toward her breasts. The man holds her legs

up and inserts his jade stalk into her jade gate. He may also stimulate her clitoris by withdrawing his jade stalk and rubbing it along her clitoris between every thrust into her. This technique is said to expel toxins from the five major organs.

6. *Flying Phoenixes.* In this technique it is the woman who does most of the moving. She lies on her back and raises her legs. Her partner is on his knees facing her, holding her legs up. He enters her, and then she begins moving. This technique benefits the marrow of the bones.

7. *Bunny Licking Its Fur.* The man lies on his back with his legs straight out in front of him. The woman mounts him, facing away from him with her head dropping down. She inserts his jade stalk into her jade gate, and then she controls the movement and the depth of his insertion. This technique is said to cure any impending illnesses.

8. *Fish Joining Scales.* The man lies on his back with his legs straight out in front of him. The woman mounts him, this time facing him. He inserts his jade stalk into her jade gate only a short way. The woman controls the movement as he lies still beneath her. Again, this technique is said to prevent illness in both the man and the woman. It is also a good practice for the man to give up the forceful yang position that he uses in some of the other techniques.

9. *Cranes with Necks Entwined.* The man is either in a squatting position or on his knees, thighs spread apart, facing the woman. She sits astride him with her arms around his neck. She inserts his jade stalk into her jade gate. He clasps her buttocks in his hands as she bounces up and down upon him. This technique is said to cure the seven illnesses.

There are other special positions that are used as a kind of medical treatment for an energetically exhausted man (see chapter 5). These usually consist of the woman sitting astride the man. It is felt that this position makes it a bit easier for the man to control his ejaculation, which allows him to hold onto vital energy and thus restore his health.

4

the poetry
of passion

The Taoists, being practical, propose that a man can begin with the most accessible energy at hand, namely the sexual attraction between men and women, and use that as a springboard to more subtle realms.

MANTAK CHIA AND MICHAEL WINN,
TAOIST SECRETS OF LOVE: CULTIVATING MALE SEXUAL ENERGY

THE POETRY OF passion begins with the premise that sexuality is as much a part of spirituality as meditation is. As we have seen, Taoists view sexuality as both sacred and healthy, if expressed in a sacred and healthy manner. Central to this view is the concept that the feminine is stronger than the masculine. The ancient Taoist ideal of the feminine nature of the earth was of paramount importance in the development of Taoist thought.

To Taoists, sex is a form of energy, and, as such, it can be used or abused. As energy, it can be used for pleasure, for communion, for communication, and for health benefits.

To the ancient Chinese, sex was an art form, as subtle and illuminating as a fine painting. As mentioned in the last chapter, the terms ancient Taoists used for sexual intercourse, sexual positions, and sexual organs are different than the ones we are used to. They are poetic and descriptive, even playful. The idea that sex was something shameful or immoral was unheard of to the ancient Chinese. It is interesting that among the extremely widespread erotic literature of ancient China (much of which was suppressed in later times by Buddhists and Confucians), we find almost no mention of sadism or masochism. Instead, much of it is spent on elaborate descriptions of varied and often highly intricate and imaginative lovers' trysts.

As for masturbation, Taoist thought is a little different than many current ideas. While Taoists would never judge masturbation from a *moral* standpoint, *energetically* it was regarded as a waste. Like orgasms during two-person sex, orgasms from masturbation are regarded as a bit different for the man than for the woman. Since the man ejaculates his essence outside his body, the idea of expelling his seed into an empty void is a waste of valuable energy. But since the woman injaculates, she doesn't lose her precious energy. Hence, masturbation to orgasm is not seen as a problem for the woman.

Oddly enough, a lot of the old wives' tales about excessive masturbation leading to blindness, memory loss, and other mental problems are upheld in Chinese medicine. The same rules apply here as with a man ejaculating too often during sex. Another problem Taoists have with masturbation is that no exchange occurs—there is no sharing, no communion with another.

On the subject of same-gender sex, Taoists would never judge homosexual practices from a moral standpoint but are more concerned about an imbalance of energy. Two yins or two yangs together make it harder to attain a proper yin/yang balance. Fortunately, there are practices that one can do to remedy potential imbalances. Both partners in a male same-sex couple need to make sure they are getting yin energy from somewhere else in their lives, such as from contact with women friends, practices that evoke the earth or yin nature in themselves, and certain yin-building herbs. Likewise, partners in a female same-sex couple need to make sure they are receiving enough yang essence. This subject is beyond the scope of this work, but suffice it to say, there are ways of achieving balance, though it does take a little extra effort.

Ancient China had a much different social structure than today's world. It was a polygamous culture in which men (who could afford it) had multiple wives and concubines. The sexual act itself often involved several partners. Indeed, some postures even require three or more participants just to perform them!

In today's culture, the idea of multiple partners complicates things not only emotionally but energetically as well. For most people, just being open and honest and energetically in tune with one other person is a big challenge; to then open the relationship to others can end up compromising everyone involved. This is not to say that it is impossible, but it would be very important to be very clear what the motives are for each party in the polygamous relationship.

Although there are currently many books and workshops available on sexual healing, some don't stress enough the responsibility that this path requires. Too often sexuality is used as power, usually over someone else. But this two-edged sword can easily be turned on one's self. This is not the way of Tao. It is not the way of spiritual integrity and unity. It only leads to disaster. The energies and powers accrued through any spiritual practice, especially sexual ones, are never to be used to dominate another or simply to benefit one's self at the expense of someone else.

Remember, sexual energy is just that, energy. It is part of the kidney system, where jing is stored and reproductive energy is produced. When we have built up lots of sexual energy without dissipating it, we are healthy, juicier, and more dynamic human beings. People around us notice this. We are more magnetic and desirable sexually but also personally and even professionally.

This great energy we have built up can be used for many things besides the sexual act itself. It can be channeled into all sorts of creative and business endeavors. We can use it to open up spiritual and psychic centers. It is up to us to use this energy in whatever way we wish.

Because it is an extremely potent form of energy, sexual energy can also be for spiritual cultivation. Many people think of spirituality as something rarified and not of this earth. They think that we are being spiritual only when we are doing "spiritual" activities, such as meditation, prayer, or ritual of some kind. Many religions discriminate against anything sexual or even sensual, as if sexuality or sensuality takes us away from our divine nature. Yet there are ancient traditions in India and China that not only honor our sexuality but also give us ways to access and experience our higher nature. To the Taoists, anything that enhances our sense of connectedness to the source, Tao, can be thought of and experienced as spiritual, including sex and relationship.

The notion that one has to be celibate in order to lead a spiritual life was not given any credence by Taoists until the later Buddhist influence crept into religious Taoism. The true natural philosophy of Tao has never felt a need to cut itself off from such a primal source of energy and delight. Hua-Ching Ni, a modern Taoist master and practitioner of Traditional Chinese Medicine, says, "Harmony between man and woman and the parallel harmony within oneself is the practical goal of Taoist spiritual learning."

Enforced celibacy disregards a particular function of the body, which in turn creates problems for the system as a whole. Medical autopsies on over a thousand Catholic priests have shown that one-third of them died of prostate complications or prostate cancer. Also, the practice of celibacy in women causes long-term congestion in the ovaries and breasts, which brings on eventual deterioration of the sexual organs and, in turn, affects other internal organs.

Another way we can use sexual energy is for self-healing. We can circulate this energy throughout our bodies, using it to heal and strengthen organs, tissue, blood, and energy pathways. The energy or chi in our body travels in very specific pathways, the two largest being up the spine and down the front of the body (*du mo* and *ren mo*). This sexual energy can be circulated not only within your own body but also between your partner and you. In this way, both partners become a living tai chi symbol, embodying the eternal dance of yin and yang in all its beauty and glory.

The most important point to remember in learning this circulation practice is to not force anything. That can lead to all kinds of energetic and health problems. In the Way of Tao we never force anything, whether it is an energetic practice or a relationship. To try to force something to happen will usually backfire on us, and the person we are so interested in relating to will be repulsed and back (or run) away!

This kind of energy circulation, besides having both health and spiritual benefits, can also affect the aging process itself.

Jing: The First of the Three Treasures

As noted in chapter 3, jing is the first of the Three Treasures, often called "the three fundamental substances," or the three energies vital to the body, health, and life. Jing is sometimes referred to as prenatal chi and is a combination of the chi of both of our parents at the moment of conception. In Taoist thought, sexual activity is not advised if both or even one of the parents is under the influence of alcohol, seriously unhealthy, or even emotionally overwrought. Conceiving a child under these conditions will result in the baby being born with poor jing and hence a poor constitution or perhaps birth defects.

Jing regulates our hormonal and reproductive systems, controls our growth throughout life, and regulates our central nervous system, including the brain, spinal cord, and bone marrow. It also governs our constitution. It is said that it takes seven mouthfuls of food to make one drop of blood. It then takes seven drops of blood to make one drop of jing. This is why jing is called "essence" and is considered extremely precious.

To the Chinese, jing, our sexual essence, governs not only our sex drive and reproductive system but our creative energy as well. Jing resides in the kidneys, and someone with strong jing will also have strong kidney energy, which translates to a solid energy body with lots of creative juices flowing.

Jing, once used up, cannot be replaced. As explained in chapter 3, men lose a lot of it with every ejaculation, and practicing optional ejaculation helps them retain their precious jing. Doing tai chi, chi gong, and other energy practices, combined with a healthy diet and lifestyle, can help both sexes live a long and healthy life.

Taoist sexual practices can be powerful tools for a greater sense of wellbeing—physical and emotional, as well as spiritual. They also engender a high level of commitment and self-responsibility. The idea is not merely to become a great sexual athlete or to use other people to enhance your own vitality. These practices instead make possible much deeper levels of trust, communion, and communication than you ever thought possible. Use them well, and you will be rewarded amply.

Energy Exchange

It is extremely important that some sort of energy exchange take place when two people are having sex. Lovemaking can include their sexual organs but must not be limited to the body only. There must be an opening of the heart and the spirit between lovers if they want to attain sacred union. Lovemaking must include a sense of honoring each other, a sense of honoring the divine presence within each other, and a sense of divine presence in each other's lives. If two people are able to really experience a sense of the divine supporting and inspiring their relationship, then they will attain the state of sacred union very easily.

Don't get too dogmatic about all of this. Taoism teaches us that flexibility is one of the most vital attributes of the realized or awakened person *(zhen ren)*. This guideline applies to many different areas of life and most especially to our sex life. By getting bogged down with trying to fit ourselves into a narrow and limiting practice, we lose the thread of Tao. We must be willing to experiment and see just what our own physical, psychic, and emotional bodies ask of us and of each other. We must be willing to tune in to what is correct or not correct in each moment. An important principle in Taoism is wu wei—not doing anything that is unnatural to one's authentic being. It also means not forcing or overdoing anything. This principle can apply to sex as well as many other things. By slowing down and becoming sensitive to each moment, to each breath, to each sigh, to each caress, we can perhaps become not only a better lover but also better able to create a deep soul connection with our beloved.

Sexuality is such a loaded and confusing world to most people today, young or old. It can be and is distorted in so many ways. If we want to have a fulfilling and even sacred union with our lover, we must be willing to listen, to learn, and to be selfless in our lovemaking. This does not mean that we do not experience any pleasure ourselves; it means that it is important to create a two-way flow so that each person alone, and both together, gets to enjoy this wonderful, powerful, and magical experience of intimacy and ecstasy.

The energetic connection between two people is very important. Many of us have met someone or even dated someone with whom we seem to share a great deal intellectually or politically, but there just does not seem to be that special spark that we are looking for. Or we may be interested in this person physically, but there still seems to be something missing. Then sometimes we meet someone for the first time, and there seems to be some sort of magnet between us, pulling us toward each other. Energetic connection is that magnet, that spark, that essential, special something that excites us and makes us want to be near a particular person in addition to, or perhaps in spite of, what might be happening on a physical or intellectual level.

This energetic attraction may not be enough for a firm foundation in love, but it is an interesting phenomenon. Sometimes we may act on this attraction, and sometimes we may not. If we are already in a committed relationship, we might just acknowledge it, either just within ourselves or even with each other. It can be a fun thing to experience and make us feel attractive and sparkly, but it need not be a thing to act upon. Emotional maturity allows us to have fun with the attraction but not feel the need to do anything about it.

On the other hand, again, energetic attraction is just as important as an emotional connection in sex. Sex without energetic attraction can be fun or exciting for a time, but if there is truly no energetic or heart connection, it will end up becoming a joyless, energy-draining affair for both people. In *Harmony: The Art of Life*, Hua-Ching Ni says, "There is no benefit in sex without love because your soul is not kindled."

When given the choice between the ordinary level of relationship, in which each person is merely marking time or putting up with less than what they actually desire or feel themselves capable of, and a life of sacred union, in which both partners are fulfilled and are actively and consciously supporting and loving each other, I believe most of us would choose the latter. Unfortunately, most people have had little or no experience with sacred union and, influenced by movies and romance novels, have an unreal and even unnatural idea of what good relationship is. All they know is that they are not living the exciting, glamorous lives that they read about and see on the big screen.

Taoists, on the other hand, are big believers in the simple and quiet lifestyle. Indeed, this is the type of lifestyle that has been attributed to the sages for thousands of years in China. Sacred union, with regular, healthy exchanges of sexual energy between the partners, is part of that lifestyle. We do not need to live high drama all the time to have an exciting exchange of energy with our partners. It is far better to have a stable yet fun relationship. Oftentimes people see the dramatic way love relationships are portrayed in movies and novels and they feel if they are not experiencing the same over-the-edge excitement, then they are missing out on something. It is important to remember that these images from movies and novels are illusory and have very little to do with reality. Constantly comparing one's relationship with these illusory images will only make one suffer.

The Power of Sexual Energy

Our sexual energy is tied in with our immune system, what the Chinese call the *wei chi* field. This is an energetic field that surrounds our body and acts as the first line of defense in our immune system. Too much sex, especially for men, with ejaculation, depletes this important chi field, leaving us open to outside influence—called "evil winds" in Chinese medicine—or for a cold or virus to enter our body.

By having strong kidney energy, we can have strong sexual energy as well as a strong immune system. Some of the things that run down our kidney energy are stress, caffeine, not enough sleep, recreational drugs, and a diet low in chi-filled foods (too much fast food or other food filled with artificial ingredients). And sexual energy itself can be a potent medicine.

In traditional Taoist herbal medicine there are three categories of herbs. One is medicinal herbs, which are used to treat various imbalances. Then there are food herbs; rich in various nutrients that our bodies need to function at a high level, they are used to supplement our diet. Lastly there are toxic herbs. These are only used in times of great need, when someone is seriously sick or even dying. These are used in very small dosages because they can be very dangerous if used improperly.

Many ancient Chinese emperors were fixated on attaining physical immortality. They were not satisfied or even particularly interested in spiritual immortality, which is what most of the Taoist practices are geared toward. They wanted to live forever *in their body*. So they scoured the provinces for Taoist sages who could cook up a "pearl of immortality" for them. Sometimes these Taoists were interested only in advancing themselves and so made all sorts of promises. Paid handsomely by the happy emperor, they would shut themselves up in their laboratory and spend months creating a pearl of immortality. They would then give it to the emperor, who would consume it. Either nothing would happen, or the pill would contain toxic herbs and minerals, and the emperor would get sick and die. Other times Taoists would be forced, upon pain of death, to create the pearl. Their results, too, would again be proven ineffective or deadly.

Sometimes a medicine can be so strong and powerful it can cause harm. This is also the case with sex. When it is not simply a case of mutual or individual masturbation, the sexual act can create or let loose powerful forces. Things can come up that sometimes people would rather not see or know. So how can we move safely and softly through this minefield experience? One way is to invest your sex life with a sense of the sacred by incorporating ritual.

Ritual: Bringing the Sacred into Sex

In most traditional cultures around the world, ritual is a big component of life. Almost every part of a people's lives—hunting, planting, fighting, religion, and sex—is accompanied by ritual. Most of us in the modern, developed world have lost touch with this part of life. Ritual can reconnect us with a very old part of ourselves, and it can reconnect us with our divine source.

Not only that, but ritual can connect you to your lover in a very powerful and rich way. It can be used in many different ways, from very simple to very complex. There are many self-help books on the shelves these days offering many kinds of tantric rituals. It is important that you find an approach or a ritual that speaks to both you and your partner. You can always create your own tantric ritual.

Bringing ritual into your love life can enhance your experience by allowing you to use the act and art of lovemaking for something beyond mere sensual pleasure. Not that there is anything wrong with sensual pleasure, but if we can magnify our experience to include a feeling of connection to the divine at the same time, why not?

One way to incorporate ritual and bring the divine into your lovemaking is to pray at the beginning of your time together. By praying I mean invoking the presence of God or the Goddess or Tao itself in your lovemaking. At the same time, try to see your partner as the Divine Feminine or the Divine Masculine. In this way, you will open yourselves to experiencing something larger and deeper than you can just by yourselves, which can make the realm of lovemaking into a more sacred and meaningful place.

It is very important to make sure the place of your lovemaking is clean and outside the normal traffic of the household. Making the bed, cleaning the floor, lighting candles, burning incense—all of these things can enhance your experience together. It's also a good way to set the scene so your lovemaking will take on the sense of the sacred.

It may sound funny, but for many women, a great kind of foreplay is for the man to clean up the kitchen! This simple act of service can help bring the woman into the place of her flowering and opening to the man. Regardless of what the movies and novels say, very few women want to be rushed into lovemaking. Going slowly, being sensitive to each other's needs or wants, spending time talking and creating a loving space within which you can move—these are all important things, and they will help to raise the vibration of your lovemaking to a high and sacred level. In lovemaking, as in chi gong and tai chi, going slowly is a key to being able to really feel the energies both within our own body and within our partner. By going too fast, we lose our place in the ever-shifting flow of the moment. When we slow down, we are able to transcend time and enter "the timeless time" of loving sexual energy.

It is also important not to get too bogged down in having things always go a particular way. We can lose the spontaneity by trying to control every moment of our lovemaking. Sometimes the flow is discovered in the moment. It would be a shame to not be able to experience it because we are always so careful to follow a script.

Coming into Harmony

As we saw in chapter 2, Taoists prize harmony very highly. Without harmony, both between us and our partner and within ourselves, there will always be conflict and problems. This harmony can be natural or nurtured. I told my partner, Shanti, early on in our relationship that I was looking for us to be in a groove with each other, instead of a rut.

Many times couples who have been together for a long time get into a very deep rut of not expecting much from the other and not inspiring each other either. Yet the old adage "familiarity breeds contempt" need not apply. Each day, each interaction, each moment is a new opportunity to inspire and aspire to higher or deeper levels of communication and communion with our partners and ourselves.

If we are committed to self-cultivation and self-growth in our mental, emotional, and spiritual lives, then we can also apply these self-cultivation practices to our relationship lives as well. Not remaining stuck in old negative ruts is both a challenge and an opportunity to grow and enjoy each other for as many years as we have with each other.

It is in creating a sense of dancing together throughout the many areas of our lives that we can create a sense of flow in our relationship. This flow can carry us through times of challenge as well as those of celebration. By "flow" I mean a sense of being in tune with each unfolding moment, our emotions and actions adjusting themselves accordingly. That is being in a groove instead of a rut.

How do we find this sense of flow, a sense of harmony? Again, it is in being flexible and sensitive to ebbs and flows of energy, attention, and intention. By both discovering and then following a flow together, both during lovemaking and in other parts of their life together, two people can avoid many difficulties and stresses. We have to go slowly and become very sensitive to each other and to our own emotional centers.

We all have our emotional buttons, and it can be extremely difficult to avoid having them punched or to avoid punching someone else's. But when our buttons or our partner's buttons are pushed, we do not make too big a deal about it. One way to do this is to practice not taking anything personally (as taught by don Miguel Ruiz in his wonderful book *The Four Agreements*). This is a very simple yet advanced practice. It can be difficult to not take personally things done or said by someone we are in a relationship with, but the dividends we will receive from the practice will pay off immensely. By not taking everything personally, we let go of our defensiveness and our need to be right in all situations. This will free up a lot of energy that we can then use to explore our relationship in a much easier, nonstressful manner.

Not taking things personally is one solution for feeling slighted or hurt, and slowing our emotional triggers is another. When we allow our emotions to flare up too quickly, we are in a reactive state and often say or do things we later regret. By taking the time to think about our responses, we can often avoid reacting too quickly.

Listening—and listening slowly—is another good way to foster harmony in our relationship. This may seem strange, but when we are truly listening to our partner and not instead thinking of what we want to say next, we can hear what they are actually saying and feeling in a much deeper way. I call this *slow listening*—really taking the time to pay deep attention to what they are trying to communicate instead of refuting or reacting to what they are saying.

Meditation practice is a good tool for slowing down our thought processes and taking us out of a reactive state into a more responsive one. Chi gong or tai chi practice is also very helpful here. The slow, deep breathing of meditation and the unhurried, even movements of these "stillness in movement" practices can slow down the usual state of our madly racing mind, allow us to experience the expansive openness of true stillness, and immeasurably slow down our emotional reaction time. Also, as you will learn in chapter 6, emotional states can be seen as energetic states, and these energetic practices can be used to access and adjust these states.

Many people blame others for all the problems in their lives, never wanting to look at how they themselves could be contributing to a difficult situation. Others get so upset every time their buttons are pushed that they live in a state of constant stress and tension.

When you find yourself in a stressful situation, take the time to reflect on just how important it is to be right or how important it is to blame the other person. Oftentimes it is possible to talk to the other person in a dispassionate way, without a lot of blaming and shaming, about what it is they are saying or doing that is upsetting to you. If you remain calm, the other person does not feel the need to immediately defend and shield themselves. By the same token, when someone points out that we have been unconscious in our acts or attitudes, we can take in that information without immediately putting up our defensive dukes. If our desire is to truly learn and grow in this lifetime, then we can take the opportunity to do just that. Sometimes, if we just can admit we were wrong, then we can move on. The question is, do we want to be right or to be open to growth, to change, and to experience ourselves as an ever-evolving person?

When our partner is in a negative or fearful state, it is important that we do not allow ourselves to be drawn into it with them. It is also often helpful to not give in to an urge to fix our partner or talk them out of whatever state they are in. This will often just make things worse. By staying present and centered within ourselves, we can give them the support they need to process their negativity or fear and move into a more positive state.

If our partner asks for our help, it is fine to plunge in and give it, but even then it is important that we respect their feelings and emotional process and not try to overlay ours onto them. Just being present and strong in our own being can often give them a safe place to go through whatever process they need to come out the other side.

It is in taking the time and attention to come into harmony, both within ourselves and with our partner, that we can find a sense of unending and dynamic flow. This will take our love relationship to ever-higher levels of joy, creativity, and harmony. It is here that the poetry of passion becomes a dance of liberation and love.

Becoming a Master or Realized Lover

Lao Tzu describes the ancient masters like this:

> The ancient achieved ones
> were masters at penetrating the subtle and profound Tao.
> They were so deep that we cannot describe them.
> They were cautious, like someone fording a frozen river.

They were vigilant, like someone who is surrounded by enemies.
They were courteous, like dignified guests.
They were ephemeral, like melting ice.
They were simple, like the uncarved block.
They were open and wide, like a valley.
They were deep, like swirling water.
(Chapter 15)

These same lines describe what we might call "the realized lover." This kind of lover does not crash their way into someone else's life, emotionally, physically, or even energetically. They move forward cautiously, as someone who is fording a frozen river and cannot always be sure of their footing. This does not mean that they are in an uptight or paranoid state; instead, all their sensory faculties are acute, and they are paying close attention to every step.

At the same time they are vigilant, like someone surrounded by enemies. Again, this does not mean being paranoid but rather in a wide-awake state; their sight, both inner and outer, is wide open, and they are aware of their surroundings.

So many romantic movies and stories talk about *falling* in love, as if that is the only way we can open ourselves to another. Perhaps walking forward in love would be a better image and a better practice. This is not to say that we cannot be excited, entranced, and inspired by someone for whom we have deep and ecstatic feelings. We can, but at the same time, we can go into a new relationship with our eyes open and all our energetic feelers out. In this way, we can often avoid a relationship that would be unhealthy or even injurious to us.

Being courteous, like dignified guests, is next. Thoughtfulness, respect, and kindness are all wonderful qualities to bring to a relationship. Often it only takes a minimum of time and energy to employ these qualities, yet doing so can make a huge difference. Simple things can mean a lot to the one we love, allowing them to feel that they are special and beloved in our eyes and heart.

The next line is a little more difficult on the surface. What does being ephemeral, like melting ice, mean exactly, and what does it mean for the realized lover? Perhaps it could mean someone is comfortable being in the moment rather than future-tripping all the time. Cultivating the ability to be fine with the present moment is a whole practice in itself. Spiritual teachers have said that the present is the point of power. If we are able to be truly present at any one moment, we can bring an enormous amount of energy and potency into that moment.

Ephemeral could also mean not holding onto a fixed image of ourselves or our partner. It is being ready to dissolve any preconceptions of self in the light of each new moment arising. Each new moment, therefore, is an opportunity for growth and change, for learning new lessons and healing old patterns of pain or fear.

By being open to change in this way, in a very immediate and dynamic fashion, we are allowing both ourselves and our partner total freedom to evolve and open ever more deeply into the Tao of intimacy and ecstasy.

Lao Tzu's next lines describe the self-realized person or sage:

> They were simple, like the uncarved block.
> They were open and wide, like a valley.
> They were deep, like swirling water.

The principle of the uncarved block, or *pu* in Chinese, is an essential element of Taoist philosophy and practice. It is the concept of the simple, uncluttered, natural man and woman and their way of life. This way of being in the world is at the heart of the teachings of Lao Tzu and Chuang Tzu. Lao Tzu says:

> Fame or self: Which is more important?
> Life or possessions: Which is greater?
> Gain or loss: Which is more harmful?
> Those who are too extreme in their love will suffer greatly.
> Those who hoard too much will suffer heavy loss.

Those who know when they have enough will not be disgraced.
Those who know restraint will not be harmed.
They will enjoy a long life.
(Chapter 44)

The ancient Taoists were not only content to live simple, natural lives but actually felt there was a solid advantage in doing so. It isn't necessary to drop out of society and live in the mountains, away from the world, in order to live a simple, natural life. What we're actually talking about is an *internal* state of simplicity and naturalness. We may be involved in all kinds of things, from running a large clinic to teaching a group of children or overseeing a complicated business. Yet none of our activities need stop us from having internal simplicity and naturalness.

It is when we allow outside pressures and complications to take up residence within us that we run into trouble and lose our sense of safety and spontaneity, which to Taoists is very serious indeed.

Tao does not judge. It does not punish, it does not condemn. We do that ourselves. As we judge, so also can we forgive ourselves and others who have wronged us through their own mistaken sense of reality. And we find in that forgiveness an even greater sense of freedom and unlimited potential—for growth, exploration, and an enlarged sense of Tao and our place in it.

Many of us read these kinds of passages from ancient texts like the *Tao Te Ching* and think, *That is all well and good for the ancient sages, but what about here and now?* This world we live in is much more complicated than Lao Tzu's, yet the ideas that he shares are still so applicable. If we keep our minds and hearts open to new adventures, new understandings, new life lessons, we too can be described as masters at penetrating the subtle and profound Tao.

The Valley Spirit

The valley is another symbol that is used a lot in Taoist teachings. In the *Tao Te Ching* we see the passage:

The valley spirit does not die.
It is called "the primal mother."
The doorway of the primal mother
is called the root of heaven and earth.
It seems to endure without end.
In drawing upon it,
it is never exhausted.
(Chapter 6)

As we saw in chapter 3, the valley represents female energy. This valley also represents Tao, in that the valley image is depthless and endless and contains all of life. The valley is the Primal Mother, the Goddess. It is through her that we reach the gateway of heaven and earth. This means that we need to connect ourselves internally to the Great Mother, the ground of our being. If we are a man, we must learn to see our lover as the form of the Goddess in our life. If we are a woman, it means to be able to experience our self as the Goddess, the source of all life.

In either case, it is through Her that we are led through the sacred gateway to the root of heaven and earth. It is through Her that we are given the grace to follow this road of intimacy and ecstasy. It is through Her grace that we are given the tools, the experiences, and the patience to do the deep soul work that it takes to reach true sacred union.

We must become as open and wide in our spirit as this depthless valley. It is only then that we will be given the sight to see what we need to do and to achieve the level of intimacy and ecstasy that we are seeking with our partner. It is in this way that we become empty vessels, waiting to become filled with grace and grit and true knowledge of what it means to be a man or woman of Tao, to be connected with our realized and authentic self, our true nature.

And lastly, we must become deep, like swirling water, as in Chuang Tzu's story of the man who not only survived plunging into the maelstrom at the bottom of the falls but also found his way back out again by becoming part of the water and following its flow.

It is when we allow ourselves to move *with* the flow of each moment rather than *against* it in an egoistic, fear-based fashion that we can not only enjoy each moment but become a graceful dancer of life, exquisitely attuned to the magic and flow of each unfolding moment. When we allow ourselves to flow with each moment, our love life, our sex life, our spiritual life all align themselves together in one great, flowing dance. Then we are the dancer and the danced, the musician and the music, the witness and the one who is witnessed, the lover and the beloved, the yin and the yang, complete in ourselves yet elegantly and gracefully in tune with our partner. This is intimacy and ecstasy in their highest forms.

5

sex as medicine

As far as Taoists are concerned, the only important distinctions regarding sexual activities are those between unhealthy and healthy habits.

DANIEL REID, *THE TAO OF HEALTH, SEX, AND LONGEVITY*

IN ANCIENT CHINA, human love, expressed through sexuality, was seen as the most potent medicine you could take. It was a kind of human herb that could cure most ailments as it restored the flow of chi, which governs our organ vitality and general immune system. During the Tang Dynasty (618–906 CE), the Art of the Bedchamber was even classified as a branch of Chinese medicine.

When we make love, there is an important and dynamic exchange of vital, health-enhancing fluids, as well as an exchange of energy. The sexual act was seen as a sort of grand dance wherein two people not only shared their own love and vitality but also enacted the cosmic dance, which enables all life to grow.

Sometimes in ancient China, when someone had a particular energetic or health imbalance, they were instructed by their physician to have sex for so many days, so many times per day. Men were told to conserve their energy during all this sex. Oftentimes the patient was also instructed on specific Taoist tantric sexual positions or positions to use for healing. For many positions, both partners, though especially the man, needed to be strong and flexible in order to maintain them. The positions were beneficial first because one needed to take care of one's own health to do them justice, and second because the positions themselves had different energetic effects.

Overall, the state of our health contributes immensely to our lovemaking. If someone is unhealthy, overweight, easily winded, weak, or distraught, their lovemaking will be affected. Exercise and diet can have a big effect on our health, including our sexual health.

As noted in chapters 3 and 4, our kidneys provide the day-to-day energy of our body. They are the pilot light under our energy system. They are also the repository of our jing, or sexual energy. If our kidney energy is weak, we will not have enough fire in our system to live up to the energy demands on our body as we go through our lives, never mind have energy for sex.

Kidney energy can be weakened by disease, stress, not enough sleep, too much mental strain, cold, and too much loss of energy during sex (hence the Taoist tantric practices for conserving sexual energy, described in chapter 3). Besides low sexual energy, kidney weakness can also manifest in low energy all around, low-back pain, insomnia, and loss of short-term memory (this is because of the kidneys' relationship with the heart, home of the spirit or shen). An extreme symptom of low kidney energy is chronic fatigue and immune deficiency syndrome (CFIDS), an increasingly prevalent disease that Western medicine has no cure for but that can be treated very successfully with Chinese herbs and chi gong. If you have weak kidney energy, herbs, acupuncture, and especially chi gong can be extremely helpful.

℘ Kidney-Strengthening Meditation

Sit on the floor, with a meditation cushion or another type of cushion under your backbone. Sit as straight as you can without being stiff, as if a string were holding your head up from above.

Closing your eyes and seeing with the mind's eye, picture a golden cloud of light hovering just above your head. See it there, all sparkly and light. Feel the warmth of it flowing down to the top of your head, to the *bai hui* point, or crown chakra. Feel its beneficent energy as it hovers there, just above your head. Then, as you inhale, draw the golden light down through your bai hui point and down into your body, a little at a time.

As you inhale, keep drawing the golden light further into your body, through the *chong mo,* or central channel, which runs right up and down through the very center of your body, from your perineum to the top of your head. Feel it flow like warm honey through your body all the way down to your lower dan tian in your lower abdomen. Feel it fill your dan tian up with good, glowing, healing light.

As you sit and experience the warm, healing light spreading out into your whole body, take a few moments to feel the light centering on your kidneys, in your lower back. Feel it gently massaging your kidneys and adrenals, cleansing and tonifying them. Feel the golden light strengthening them. Feel them getting stronger as you feel the warmth spread all over your lower back. Spend some time seeing and feeling this. You can imagine the golden light or healing chi repeatedly coming down from above your bai hui, flowing down the central channel, and then flowing into your lower back and into your kidney area. You may even feel a sense of warmth in your lower back as you do this.

When you feel done, slowly bring your consciousness back to the outer world by briskly rubbing your

palms together thirty-six times, laying them on your
lower back, and breathing their warmth into your
kidneys for nine breaths. Then briskly rub your kidney
area thirty-six times or more with your palms, circling
in an upward and outward direction.

Just as chi gong practice was originally designed to strengthen our chi
(vital life force) and bring our energies into harmony so we could then
go on to deeper spiritual cultivation, sex can also be a tool to bring
our energies into harmony—both the energies within ourselves and
between us and our partner, in order that we may be healthier, both
physically and energetically, and so we can go deeper into our own
spiritual practice. In this way, lovemaking can be seen as a medicine of
the highest order!

If a man's energy is weak, then he can use gentle, relaxed lovemaking
as a kind of tonic, as long as he is careful to retain his seed. The endorphins that are released into our bloodstream while two people make
love can have a very rejuvenating effect, and the exchange of energy
between partners can also be very healing.

Going Slowly

When engaging in sex as an energetic healing practice, be sure to go
slowly and relax into each moment as it unfolds. Experience your lovemaking as a deep sharing of two hearts and bodies. Bathe in the sensual
pleasure of touching your partner as well as being touched by them.
Drink deeply of their kisses and allow yourself to relax into the present moment as being the only moment. Use this as an opportunity to
really show your partner how much you love them. Instead of being
focused on your own pleasure the whole time, be sure and spend some
time enjoying the pleasure that you can give to them. By freely giving
at this time, you will reap the benefits of feeling your lover open him-
or herself to you. By not focusing on yourself, you can better feel how

your lover is feeling. By focusing on your partner, you can give the gift of selflessness, a wonderful trait in a lover.

It is in taking your time to be together, to open to each other, to receive from each other that your lovemaking will truly be a healing experience. Quickies may be fun once in a while, but if you really want to experience how deeply healing sex can be, it is important that you give yourselves a little timeless time. If you have other things to do during the rest of the morning or afternoon or evening, then decide ahead of time how much time you can give to your lovemaking. This way you will not have to be watching the clock the whole time. Then allow yourselves to really relax and sink into the feeling of timeless time, where moments glide by like hours and an hour's time can feel like forever.

Get rid of glaring lights. Make sure the pets are outside the room. Light candles and incense, put on relaxing, sensual music. Then be sure to spend some time really looking at and listening to each other. So much of the time when we see love scenes in a movie the two lovers crash into each other, breathing heavily and ripping each other's clothes off and falling to the bed or the floor or else bumping into the walls and furniture. By instead starting slowly and really tuning into each other first, you will find that you naturally flow into a smooth and deep sharing that is just as exciting, if not more so, than banging into furniture—and definitely better for you if you or your partner's energy is depleted!

When a man is fatigued or ailing, his impulse may be to avoid lovemaking because he feels he can't be as hot and fiery as he thinks men are supposed to be to satisfy their lovers. A man or a woman may not want to risk "failing" at sex by not being able to come to orgasm. By opting out of sex for these reasons, we may be missing the other benefits of lovemaking—the energetic exchange, the physical contact, the emotional intimacy—which can all be very healing and exactly what we need to begin recovering our diminished energy. If you or your partner is in this situation, take the opportunity to try slower lovemaking that is focused on the sensual details of the moment and not focused on getting to orgasm. You may well find the experience to be even more satisfying than sex with orgasms, as well as giving you the healing and rejuvenation you need.

Talking a little—perhaps about what happened for each of you during the day or about what you have been thinking about or feeling in the hours leading up to lovemaking—is a way to slow down and connect, energetically and emotionally, before beginning to connect physically. Be sure and look into each other's eyes a little and really connect emotionally when your partner is speaking. Show that you are genuinely interested in hearing what your partner wants to share. Feel free to share some of your own thoughts and feelings so that your partner does not feel that you are just humoring them. While it is often much easier—for men especially—to focus just on the physical aspect of lovemaking, many people want and need to feel a strong emotional bond with their lover in order to really surrender to their lover and their lovemaking. If you find it difficult to think about anything more than the physical during sex, think about this for a moment: Is it really true that all you want is physical pleasure with a momentary release at the end? Sure, sensual pleasure is great and allowing yourself to surrender to a moment of fully letting yourself go into your partner is also great. But if that is all you ever experience from lovemaking, you are missing out on so much!

All of this is not to say that each time you make love you need to follow all these recommendations. There is always room for improvisation and being creative on your own. Sometimes you may find yourselves flowing into lovemaking after waking up in the morning or when you think you are saying goodnight or just because the mood strikes you. It is important not to get bogged down with so many rules that your lovemaking becomes stilted or too formal. But if, at least some of the time, you explore bringing a little attentiveness and intention to your lovemaking, you can experience just how deep two people can go. You can feel just what it is like to make your lovemaking a sacred act, a form of true medicine, for the heart and soul as well as for the body.

It is by letting our lovemaking become a dance—sometimes danced slowly and deliciously, sometimes danced wildly and boldly, and sometimes like easing back into an old and familiar tune—that we can find ourselves in the pure and holy place of healing and a place of intimacy and ecstasy.

૨♣ Expansion Breathing Exercise

Here's a simple yet powerful chi gong exercise that will allow you to experience the expansion of your own personal being or energy (chi) so when you are in the midst of lovemaking, you can allow your own energy to expand and join your lover's. Both of you can then expand your combined energy until you are enveloped by it. You will be able to fill the room with your energy, creating a living yin/yang, and be able to bask in the glow of your shared energy bodies.

Sit or lie comfortably, with eyes closed. Feel your abdomen expand as you inhale and contract as you exhale. At the same time, feel your sense of yourself expand. Feel your chi expand in a circle or bubble to just outside your skin. Inhale and exhale a few times, feeling your chi and your sense of self expand. Then allow your chi to expand even more until it fills the room you are in. Be with that for a few moments. Then allow it to expand to encompass the entire building you are in. After a few more moments, allow it to expand to fill the entire town or city you are living in. Then allow it to expand to cover the entire country you live in. Next, allow it to expand to cover the entire planet. Then, allowing it to expand even more, let it extend to the outer reaches of space, as far as your imagination can take you. Feel your being expanding in this way, until you experience your sense of self as huge and vast as the universe itself.

Go slowly and really try to feel what this sense of expansion is like. An old saying in chi gong is that the chi can go as far as the mind can imagine. It may seem strange at first to imagine yourself as a planetary being, but there is a part of us, our original Tao nature, that is just that.

Then, slowly and deliberately, retract your sense of self, your chi body, back to the size of the planet, the country, the city, the room, and lastly, back into your own body.

Love Potion #9

It is interesting to note that while good health is a big prerequisite for a satisfying sex life, deeply nourishing intimate sex with a loving partner is very good for our health. This is not only an ancient Taoist belief but also a fact supported by modern Western medical science. The reason lies with the many and varied chemical and hormone interactions within our body.

One of the hormones at play is oxytocin, which is released during and after lovemaking. Oxytocin is sometimes called the "cuddling hormone," as it promotes feelings of affection and nurturing. This is why most people feel an urge to cuddle and bask in the afterglow of lovemaking. It can also be found in mother's milk and released when a woman gives birth, helping with the bonding process between mother and child. It is secreted in the pituitary gland and, in men, stimulates the prostate, leading to more intense orgasms. Oxytocin is also a natural sedative and can lead to deeper sleep once it has been released during orgasm. It also lowers blood pressure and provides stress relief.

Another effect of oxytocin is pain relief. When released during orgasm, it can relieve many types of pain, including pain from headaches, menstrual cramps, and overall body aches.

The next group of helpful chemicals is endorphins. These are a group of neurotransmitters that bind to opiate receptor sites in our brain to naturally relieve pain and stress. Endorphins are famous for their ability to fill us with a sense of wellbeing and relaxation and are sometimes called the body's natural opiates, as they can give us a sense of euphoria. They have pain-relieving properties similar to those of morphine.

Some studies have shown that a small amount of growth hormone is released during lovemaking. It may be that this hormone is responsible for the more youthful appearance of those who are regularly sexually active.

Another hormone affected by lovemaking is adrenaline. Adrenaline activates the sympathetic nervous system, increasing our heart rate and dilating arteries to increase blood flow to our muscles during sex. During lovemaking, increased amounts of adrenaline are released from the adrenal glands, amplifying the circulatory system with each heart contraction.

Indeed, studies have found that frequent intercourse is associated with lower diastolic blood pressure in each partner. Some researchers say that having sex twice or more times a week reduces the risk of a fatal heart attack or stroke by half, compared to having sex less than once a month. In other words, sex can dramatically improve our cardiovascular health.

Erectile dysfunction may be caused by circulatory problems. To produce an erection, the penis must fill with blood. Blocked arteries, high blood pressure, and other cardiovascular issues can interfere with that process. Exercise, which keeps the heart and arteries healthy, can reduce the risk of this problem. Research has shown that for men over fifty, those who are physically active have stronger erections and a 30 percent lower risk of impotence than those who are inactive.

Lovemaking encourages the flow of testosterone, which strengthens bones and muscles and even helps transport DHEA (dehydroepiandrosterone), an important hormone involved in the body's immune system. DHEA also helps repair tissue, improve cognition, and keep skin healthy, and it even works as an antidepressant. Frequent sex has also been linked to increased levels of an antibody called immunoglobulin A, which protects against colds and other kinds of infections.

Another chemical action released during lovemaking is phenylethylamine, which, in turn, triggers the release of dopamine in the pleasure centers of our brain. This chemical is released during sex and peaks at orgasm. Interestingly, it is also one of the chemicals found in dark chocolate.

Serotonin regulates our moods and is essential to our libido and sexual arousal. During orgasm, serotonin is released into our brains, where it acts as a natural antidepressant. (Many prescription antidepressants work by pumping up serotonin levels in our brain.)

Prolactin is another hormone that is produced by lovemaking. This causes stem cells in the brain to develop new neurons in our brain's olfactory bulb, its smell center, improving our sense of smell.

Of course there are a great many muscles involved in lovemaking, including those of the pelvis, thighs, buttocks, arms, and neck. Sixty-year-olds who exercise frequently have sex as often and experience as much sexual pleasure as people decades younger. Sex itself can be quite a workout, and if we exercise at other times, we have more energy for sex. One study found that women who exercise frequently become aroused more quickly and are able to reach orgasm faster and more intensely than women who do not exercise.

As mentioned earlier, sex can have many effects on cardiovascular health. When we begin to make love, our respiration and heart beat rates increase. This is because our bodies are getting ready to send more blood (and chi) to our genitals. As we proceed, there is a whole cascade of hormones that get released, including adrenaline, noradrenaline, prolactin, DHEA, and testosterone, many of which have cardioprotective effects. Not only that, but during sex, a fresh supply of blood is pumped though our body, providing the organs with a healthy dose of oxygen and ridding our body of old waste products. The body also burns off 150 calories during every half hour of sex.

Orgasm itself involves a complex interaction between three systems of our body: the vascular system, the nervous system, and the endocrine system.

An interesting study seems to support the Taoist theory of yin/yang nourishing one another during sex. This study found that women whose male partners did not use condoms were less susceptible to depression than those whose partners did. One idea about the cause of this has to do with the hormone prostaglandin, found only in male semen. When absorbed by the female through her genital tract, this male hormone modulates the woman's own female hormones. In other words, it is the yang essence that the yin female is drinking through her vagina that has this effect of combating depression.

ಌ Sexual Strength Exercise

Here's a simple exercise you can do to improve your sexual strength. It works for both men and women.

Sit or lie down, and let yourself relax completely. While inhaling, draw your pelvic floor up. (Men will feel their testicles rising as well.) To begin with, you can imagine you are urinating, and you want to stop. (You can also practice this action while actually urinating.)

Gently pull up on your entire pelvic floor and hold it just a few seconds at first, then for thirty seconds or more once you have gotten comfortable with the exercise. Remember to always be gentle with yourself and never force anything.

This practice uses the pubococcygeus muscle, or PC muscle, which stretches from your pubic bone to your tailbone. By strengthening and toning this muscle, you can intensify your orgasm. It will also give men greater control over their ejaculations. Most women know this exercise as "the Kegel exercise." It not only allows women to enjoy greater pleasure during lovemaking, but it also minimizes the risk of incontinence later in life.

For men, pulling up gently on the pelvic floor while thrusting into his partner will intensify his sensations. Pulling up on the pelvic floor a little more forcefully will stop an impending ejaculation. It will massage the prostate gland as well.

For many people, being in a love relationship is a deeply healing experience. At the same time, a relationship that has outgrown its purpose or that is very inharmonious can actually make us sick. Ongoing stress can cause all sorts of problems. Be sure you are not holding on to a stressful relationship out of habit or fear.

6

the energetics of emotions

*The difficulty of being spiritual is not because you
are not moral enough, or you are not spiritual enough,
but because you are captive to your emotions.*

HUA-CHING NI, *MOONLIGHT IN THE DARK NIGHT*

TAOISTS VIEW EMOTIONS in a very different way than we do in
the West. To the Chinese, emotions are seen as energetic states, not merely
psychological ones. We can work to balance, detoxify, and strengthen our
organs, which will, in turn, balance and harmonize our emotions.

When speaking of organs in Chinese medical tradition, it is important to understand that we are not speaking of the actual physical organ
but rather the energetic qualities attributed to it. Organs are looked at
as function rather than form. Therefore, when a traditional Chinese
physician says you have weak kidneys, it doesn't mean you're a candi-
date for dialysis. It simply means the energetic quality of your kidneys
is weak, thereby adversely affecting the other organs that are paired
with or related to the kidneys, such as the adrenal glands.

In Taoist thought, the human body is a microcosm of the entire
universe. Our organs, also called "heavenly orbs" or "celestial spheres,"

are analogous to, and even directly related to, the heavenly bodies of the solar system. They are regarded as living, pulsing, vibrating centers of energy within our bodies. These links between the human physical body and the heavenly bodies in space explains why astrology played such a major role in classical Chinese medicine.

Understanding emotions in terms of energy and knowing the correlations between emotions and the body helps us better address the emotions that inevitably arise in our relationship with our partner.

Our Emotional Bodies

Each organ, besides having an energetic or medical aspect in the body, carries a particular emotional resonance. And it has relationships with a particular time of the year, a color, an element, and a taste or flavor, among other things. These associations are part of the *wu xing* system, often translated as "the Five Elements," but better translated as "the Five Transformational Phases."

Kidneys

In Chinese medicine, the kidneys function together with the adrenal glands. They govern urinary function and the sexual and reproductive organs and also house the jing, which is responsible for the growth and development of the body, as well as our sexual energy. They are the source of the body's resistance and endurance, and of physical, emotional, and spiritual tenacity. They are the seat of willpower.

The kidneys are a source of much of our body's day-to-day energy. They can be thought of as the pilot light under the furnace. If the flame is too low, the entire energetic heating system will perform inadequately. Chronic fatigue conditions are usually a sign of weak kidney energy.

The emotion associated with the kidneys is that of willpower or "backbone"; the negative aspect of this emotion is fear. Kidney problems contribute to excessive fear or anxiety, such as panic attacks and night sweats. The element associated with the kidneys is water. The color is blue-black. The season is winter. The kidneys are associated with the direction south, and their totem animal is the black turtle (or sometimes the turtle and snake entwined).

Spleen

When the Chinese refer to the spleen, they include the stomach by definition, since the two are paired in the process of digestion. Weak spleen energy means weak digestion and thus poor absorption of chi from the food we eat.

The element associated with the spleen is earth, the color is yellow, and the season is Indian summer. The direction is the center of the circle. The emotional tone associated with the spleen is empathy, though in its negative sense it becomes worry or self-absorption. The tendency to go over and over a problem searching for an elusive solution is regarded as a sign of spleen weakness. The totem animal is the yellow dragon.

Liver

Besides filtering toxins, the liver is the storehouse of the blood in that it regulates the amount of blood in the vessels and stores a large amount of blood at night. It also regulates movement within the body, such as the flow of chi, blood, hormones, lymph, and even emotions.

The liver governs our ability to move gracefully through the challenges of our life. The element associated with the liver is wood (of plants, grasses, and trees), the color is green (the green of freshly growing grass and other plants), and the season is spring (the season of new beginnings and outward expansion). The emotional state associated with the liver is free-flowingness. If the liver gets backed up, too toxic, or "too tight," then feelings of anger will rush up out of nowhere. The totem animal is the green dragon.

Lungs

The lungs dominate the chi and respiration. The element associated with the lungs is gold (or metal), the color is white, and the season is fall. The positive emotion is courage, while the negative emotion is grief. (It is believed that excessive or unexpressed grief can injure the lungs.) The totem animal is the white tiger.

Heart

Besides controlling blood circulation, the heart is said to house the shen, or spirit. Problems with the heart can take the form of purely medical ones, such as cardiac problems and circulatory problems. Problems with the shen aspect of the heart come under what is called "disturbed shen or spirit" and can include mental illness, memory loss, insomnia, and unclear thinking. The heart it also thought of as the seat of consciousness, as well as conscious thinking. Indeed, the mind is said to live in the heart. So when Taoist people talk about the cognitive mind, they are talking about the heart as well.

The element associated with the heart is fire, the color is red, and the season is summer. The emotions associated with the heart are joy, creativity, and expansion. The negative emotion is hysteria, or joy taken to an extreme (in an unbalanced way). The totem animal is the red phoenix.

Again, it is important to remember that what we are speaking of is something quite other than the Western anatomical organ.

Emotional Imbalance Is Energetic Imbalance

What those of us in the West would think of as emotional or even psychological problems are seen as energetic imbalances in Taoist medicine. For example, a disturbed shen, or disturbed spirit, can cause all sorts of mental problems. Instead of sitting down and going over the patient's childhood history, the Taoist doctor will treat the shen through the heart meridian. Different things that can cause disturbed shen are stress, an unhealthy lifestyle, too much thinking, and too strong emotions. And while it may be hard for us in the West to believe that too much happiness can be problematical, too much joyful exuberance (joy taken to an extreme) can damage the spirit of the heart.

There are other things that can cause problems with the shen/heart, such as imbalances in other parts of the body, especially the kidneys or adrenals (a common problem in Western fast-paced society). In the holistic worldview of Taoist medicine, all the systems of the body affect each other. One system being out of balance can throw some other part out of balance as well. The important thing to remember is that it is possible to work with these kinds of problems through the energetics of the body and its various organs.

Fear is a big problem that many people are dealing with. We are not talking about sensible fear here but the nameless dreads that come up in the middle of the night and are accompanied by night sweats or the sudden onset of panic attacks. These are signs that your kidney energy is weak and thus your adrenals are as well. Getting better rest, taking herbs and medicinal foods to strengthen the kidneys, and doing chi gong practices all work well for this problem, though rejuvenating the kidneys can take some time if they are very weak.

Depression is another big problem in the West. One of the ways Chinese medicine regards depression is as liver stagnation. This means that the free-flowingness of the liver energy is stuck. As a result, the person feels stuck in a negative flow in their life. If the stuck energy gets too tight, then the other aspect of depression will result—anger. If the liver is overheated, through consuming too much alcohol or other toxic substances, it can cause heat to rush up to the head, bringing with it feelings of anger. (This is also why many alcoholics have red faces, often with broken blood vessels in their noses.)

Too much self-absorption is a problem for the spleen. The habit of going over and over each little problem or decision is a sign of spleen weakness. The opposite is also true: this habit of dwelling on problems will also damage the spleen energy. It is interesting to note that energetic imbalances in various organ systems can cause all sorts of problems. At the same time, too much activity in one of these unhealthy patterns can cause problems in the organ systems.

Our spleen is where we feel our connection to the earth and to what Lao Tzu calls "the ten thousand beings," or all of life. If we do not have a sense of groundedness or rootedness to the earth and to our own inner being, we will end up having spleen problems. The rooting practice offered in chapter 11 will help with this, as will being careful with your diet and not eating too many sweets. The spleen likes a little sweetness but not too much!

Overindulgence in any one emotion can cause imbalances. Too much grief or too much unexpressed grief, for example, can both cause problems with the lungs. The Taoist model is for moderation in all things, even emotions. Often people give themselves all sorts of permission to indulge in wild emotions, thinking that they are being "real" or "passionate" people. What they are really doing is setting themselves up for all sorts of physical and energetic problems.

People may wonder, how can too much joy be a problem? It is when it is carried to such an extreme state that the person loses their center and their sense of being grounded in their being. Their joy may be so over the top that it edges into hysteria. On the other hand, we all know people who laugh somewhat hysterically all the time, but it is clear that they are not happy people. It is a kind of false gaiety that they are caught up in; the joy does not come from deep in their heart.

Revising Our Understanding of Emotions

What does all of this have to do with the Tao of intimacy and ecstasy, you may ask. It is when emotions flare up or even take over our lives that we feel afraid, uprooted, or angry. We may blame our partner or take ourselves too seriously (a grave mistake for a Taoist indeed). But in understanding that what we think of as emotional states are often energetic states, we can seek the kind of help we need to bring ourselves into balance and not get too caught up in the psychological or intellectual approach.

Also, when we see these emotional/energetic states in our partner, we can avoid getting too psychological about them and instead understand that many times negative emotions are caused by various organ systems being out of balance. It is actually much simpler to address unbalanced or extreme emotions from an energetic standpoint rather than a psychological one. It may take a combination of Chinese herbal medicine, acupuncture, meditation, visualization, and chi gong practice to affect great change in your life, but doing so can be worth it if your relationship with your partner or with yourself is suffering.

If you feel a lot of brain fuzziness and have trouble remembering anything; if you wake up in the night with feelings of panic; if you feel filled with grief but cannot express it; if you feel ungrounded and are having trouble digesting your food, as well as the experiences of your life; if you are getting angry and losing your temper with your partner much more often than usual; if your feelings of joy and creativity seem blocked, think about looking into Chinese medicine or doing some chi gong practices, such as the ones in this book, to bring yourself into balance.

Understanding the basic energetic functions of the various organ systems of the body can also bring a sense of objectivity. It is when we are caught up in seemingly uncontrollable passions or fears that we can lose sight of who are and what we want from our partner. This is not to say that all extreme emotions are physically or energetically based, but you would be amazed how many are. A little objectivity and knowledge about how to bring ourselves into balance can help us immensely on our quest for the Tao of intimacy and ecstasy!

✤ Organ-Balancing Meditation

Here is a visualization and meditation practice that you can do to help balance your emotions.

Sitting quietly, breathe gently and slowly, from the belly. Close your eyes.

Imagine a cloud of light hovering just above your head. It can be a billowy, fluffy cloud or a sparkling cloud of energy or whatever other form feels right to you. Feel it floating there, just above your head, for a moment or two.

Then let it slowly sink down through the top of your head, down the right side of your body, and settle just below and underneath the rib cage—at the liver. Here it becomes a rich green—the green of spring, of new growth, of expansion and free-flow-ingness. The element of the liver is wood, the wood of plants, grasses, and trees. It is the season of spring, of new beginnings, and of outward expansion.

The liver, besides acting as a filter for the toxins in our system, regulates movement within the body. The ability for blood, chi, and even emotions to move freely through the system is governed by our liver. So too it governs our ability to move freely through our emotions and our life.

Picture your liver as rich green, supple, and flexible, better able to help you move through the changes and challenges in your life. Picture yourself as the rich new growth of spring—resilient, strong, and supple. Bring your positive attention to your liver and give thanks for the wonderful job it does for you every day.

Now the energy cloud moves up to your chest, to your heart. Here it becomes a bright, vibrant red. Red is the color of summer, when all of life is at its peak. It is a joyous, creative time, when the bright sun shines mightily down upon us all. Feel this season in your heart as the red cloud pulses slowly in your chest. The element of the heart is fire—the fire of controlled passion and creativity.

The heart's job is to keep the blood moving freely throughout the body. It is also the home of the shen, or spirit. It is that which makes us human, that which gives us consciousness. Picture this vibrant red cloud lying lightly on your heart, filling it with joy and purpose, openness, and creativity—the positive emotions of the heart.

Sit and relax for a little bit and allow yourself to feel this joy deep within you. In Taoist practice, it is said that "chi follows *yi,*" or energy follows the mind. Wherever you put your attention is where the energy will go. It is important to always keep our thoughts positive and supportive, so this will be the kind of energy we will attract and create within ourselves.

Bring your positive attention to your heart and thank it for the wonderful job it does for you night and day, every night and day.

Next we move down to the left side of our abdomen to our spleen and stomach area. Here the cloud turns to a vibrant, earthy yellow. The spleen element is earth; its season is Indian summer, or as observed in ancient times, the pause between seasons. The spleen is the grounding force in our being.

The spleen helps our digestion, extracting the chi from what we eat. It also helps us digest our experiences.

Take a little time to allow yourself to feel your empathy, the positive emotion of the spleen, and your connection to the earth and all living things. Sink your roots deep into the earth; draw up the pure yin chi found there and let it fill you up, from the bottoms of your feet to the top of your head. Bring your positive attention to your spleen and give it thanks for working so well for so long.

Now move the cloud up to your chest and into your lungs. When it reaches your lungs, it turns bright white. It hovers there, within your lungs,

filling them with vital, healing energy. The corre-
sponding season is autumn, the time when growing
things are beginning to close up shop for the long
sleep of winter. The element is gold or metal.

The lungs rule the respiration, our ability to
extract oxygen and other nutrients, as well as chi,
from the air around us. And they govern our *wei,* or
protective chi, guarding us against outside evils or
attacking forces like colds and flus. Picture then, your
lungs becoming strong and healthy, expanding easily
with each breath, sending out the protective chi to all
parts of your body. Picture each cell expanding and
contracting as you breathe deeply through the belly.

Feel the positive emotions of the lungs—courage and the ability to surrender deeply to each
moment—as this bright white cloud of energy lies
loosely upon your lungs. Bring positive attention to
your lungs for allowing you to breathe in and out
thousands of times a day.

Next move the cloud to your lower back, to the
kidneys. Here the cloud turns a deep blue-black. The
element is water; the season winter, the time when
earth energy is dormant and deep. The kidney-adrenal
area is the seat of your will. It also is the source of your
day-to-day energy, the pilot light beneath your furnace.

Here we store our sense of will and determination.
Feel your willpower and the ability to deal with your
life in a positive and creative fashion.

Sit for a few moments and allow yourself to
breathe deeply into your kidneys and lower back.
Each breath fills the kidneys with powerful chi so
they will be able to hold you up, both in your daily
life and in all your endeavors.

Our kidneys are where we store our prenatal chi, or jing, which is very important to our physical and mental development. They are also the repository of our generative or sexual energy. Because the very pulse of life starts here, it is important that you work on creating strong kidney energy and not dissipate it through a self-abusive lifestyle.

Bring positive attention to your kidneys and express deep gratitude for them working so tirelessly for you throughout your lifetime.

From here, either you can go back to the liver and cycle the cloud through all the organs again, or you can let the energy cloud ascend back up through your head.

Do this practice daily or whenever you feel a need to get in touch with those qualities that the organs represent. In time you will become sensitized to the health, the vitality, and the inner integrity of not only your inner organs but also your emotions.

opening the heart

In Taoist learning and teaching, we like to build
the mind and heart to have depth like a mountain valley.
This is termed having "deep-valley heartedness."

HUA-CHING NI, *MOONLIGHT IN THE DARK NIGHT*

WITHOUT AN OPEN heart, without a heart as deep as a valley, we are not able to surrender to and extend toward another. Without an open heart, we are not able to hear the music of another's heart. Without an open heart, we are not able to heal both ourselves and our partner. Without an open heart, we are not able to plumb the depths of our own being and bring light into the dark places we find there. Without an open heart, we are not able to find the strength that we need to truly attain intimacy and ecstasy.

Opening the heart means healing the heart. It also means developing a kind heart. Without these two things, we will be lost in the often-confusing world of feeling and emotion and will not be able to live up to the full potential of true sacred union.

Developing a Kind Heart

Developing a kind heart begins with compassion. What do we mean by compassion? It might mean our sense of shared suffering. It must also include a sense of sharing in the joy of others, for it is sharing such primal experiences and feelings that binds us, that gives us our sense of belonging to something larger than what we experience as individuals. It is in that shared sense of belonging that we may find some relief from, and perhaps even some solution to, the human dilemma.

We all want to be happy. That is a basic drive and need of the human race. It is also true that no one likes to suffer. But life in the material world has its share of suffering built into it. And while joy is easy to share, suffering often isolates us and cuts us off from what we need the most—the comfort and presence of others of our own kind, those others we share our suffering with, whether we realize it or not, simply by being alive. To develop a kind heart, we must share our suffering as well as our joy.

Lao Tzu says that we must treat favor and disgrace as the same thing. In other words, when things are going badly for us, we must remember that the seed of change is inherent in any situation, just as in the yin/yang symbol, the seed of one concept is inherent in the other. As we saw in chapter 2, when we explore yin/yang, change is inevitable. Conversely, when things are going really well for us, we must always keep in mind that things can change or even reverse in a moment. This does not mean that we need to live in fear; just that when we are on an up cycle, we must always remember not to get so carried away with ourselves that we are crushed when the downward cycle begins.

It is by opening our heart, as deeply and widely as possible to each unending moment, that we are able to flow with the challenges that life offers us. We must cultivate a deep sense of gratitude for all that we have in our life—our relationships, our work, our health, our family—whatever blessings we can recognize in our life. *With gratitude comes grace.* This means that if we approach our lives with a sense of gratitude and openness, our lives will become richer and more fulfilling.

To really experience and express this feeling of gratitude, it can help to give thanks daily for the meals we eat, the time we get to spend with loved ones, the fact that we have been given another day of life in this beautiful world. Get in the habit of blessing your food before each meal or begin each day with a brief prayer of thanks for another day of life. Even if you are living in dire circumstances, there is always something to be thankful for.

Taking the time to acknowledge what is good about our relationship, what we treasure, what we appreciate in our beloved will instill in us a sense of grace and gratitude, which will, in turn, help open our hearts, not to mention make our love life much more fulfilling. It is very important to express verbally to our partner what we appreciate about them and our relationship, as well as show them in ways, both small and large, just how precious they are to us.

Be thankful as well for the challenges of your life. These are the experiences that will help you to grow. By using the negative experiences in your life as medicine, as opportunities to grow in character and depth, you will be able to use all the myriad experiences, both good and bad, of your life as self-cultivation.

Life is full of challenges, frustrations, object lessons, unwanted surprises, and other types of suffering. Taoists, as well as those on other spiritual paths, understand that suffering is inevitable. It is just part of life. We cannot escape suffering. It comes with the territory of life. Even if we hide ourselves away in a far-off mountain, as many Taoist recluses and masters have done, we will still not escape suffering in its myriad and often subtle forms.

If we truly wish to cultivate a kind, open heart, we must learn especially how to let personal attacks or injustices fall away from us as soon and as lightly as possible. The Buddha once said that expressing anger toward someone is like picking up a stick of burning wood. Not only does it harm the person it is thrown at, but it also burns the person who picks it up.

The human heart is a wondrous thing. In many traditions, it is the seat of the soul itself. To the Taoists, the heart is the center of the mind and our shen, or spirit. To develop a kind heart is to invoke our humanness, that ability we all have to envision and share deeply in the reality and existence of others. Inherent in developing a kind heart is the ability to open as deeply as we are able to, moment by moment, to a quality of feeling that enables us to not only experience our own suffering or joy but also that of everyone else we share space with on our beloved planet Earth.

Lao Tzu says:

> Those who value their own wellbeing
> equally with the rest of the world,
> can be trusted with the world.
> Those who love their life as if it were the whole world,
> will be trusted with all things under heaven.
> *(Chapter 13)*

"Those who are at one with loss," says Lao Tzu, "experience loss willingly." What if instead of experiencing loss as a blow, we can find a way to experience loss as an opportunity for something else to come through? We may think we are so in love with someone that we will die without them, only to find, after they leave, that we can not only continue to live but can also go forward into our life in a new and exciting way. When we are one with loss and experience a loss willingly, then it will cease *being* loss and instead become another step on the road to coming to know our true or authentic self.

Everything is relative, say the Taoists. Lao Tzu says:

> Under heaven everyone knows that
> the existence of beauty
> depends on the existence of ugliness.
> Everyone knows that the capacity of kindness
> depends on the existence of the unkind.
> Existence and nothingness are mutually born,
> difficulty and ease complete each other,
> long and short shape each other,

tall and short rest upon each other,
sound and music harmonize each other,
before and after follow one another.
(Chapter 2)

With this quote, we see that what we might think of as solid, unchanging truth is really only true in relation to something else. How do we know we are happy? Partly by comparing a happy time to a time when we were not happy. How do we know what is the right thing to do? Partly by remembering when we did something else that caused ourselves or someone else suffering.

Perhaps if we were not always comparing—comparing situations, people, activities—to what we think of as the right situation, person, or activity, we would actually find ourselves in a place that feels free of comparisons. This, the ancient enlightened ones say, is Tao. Perhaps then we could relax and just be with that situation, person, or activity in a completely natural and nonjudgmental way and find that what we may have thought of as a problem is not actually a problem at all.

Taoism teaches that all life is made up of change—change within change. One day we're ahead, the next we feel behind. One day we're happy, the next sad. It is in our endless quest for that unattainable moment of fixation, of having it our way once and for all, that leads us to frustration and despair.

Tao itself is much larger than we can ever imagine. It contains all that we know and all that we may never know. It is there that we have our beginning and our so-called end. It is in that endless becoming that we may find some sense of respite and rest from the suffering of the world.

For that very Tao that keeps the heavens in place and causes the green growing things to sprout forth from the earth, year after year, is also contained in us. It lives there, sometimes quietly, sometimes stormily, but nevertheless eternal, rooted in our very being.

I'd like to share a poem of mine called "Healing the Heart."

Healing the heart—
means opening the heart,
means softening the heart,
means strengthening the heart,
means breaking the heart.
Opening the heart—
means letting go,
means realizing
all that we don't know
and some that
we never will,
means giving up
who we think we are
and who we think
we ought to be,
means opening to experience
and all that it contains,
means forgetting
our small selves
in order that
our higher selves
can come through.
Softening the heart—
means letting in the light
to fill up the shadows
and give them form
and substance,
means letting in
the darkness too,
the fear, the sadness,
and the pain,
means accepting ourselves
unconditionally,

in all our glory
and in all our
humble pride,
means being open
to chance
to growth,
and to miracles.
Strengthening the heart—
means nurturing ourselves,
and in that nurturing
being able
to nurture others
so that they too
may strengthen their hearts,
means living our life
in all its manifestations,
both "good"
and "bad,"
means dwelling
as much as possible
in the stillness
and loving emptiness
of the universe,
the all embracing
Mother Tao,
means being humble
and accepting help
on a regular basis,
means giving to others
what we ourselves need.
Breaking the heart—
means allowing ourselves
to be hurt

to suffer,
to cry out
in the dark
and lonely night,
means allowing ourselves
to be comforted
in times of need,
means letting the cracks
show in our armor,
the better for the light
to shine in,
means at last
to be willing,
to give of ourselves
to ourselves
and to those others around us,
those others,
who are also in need,
in pain, afraid and alone,
means to forgive ourselves
and those others
who have hurt us
who have taught us,
who are in pain themselves,
whose own hearts
are breaking,
and mending
and breaking again.
Healing the heart then,
with the four treasures—
opening, softening,
strengthening and breaking,
the path to wholeness,

and wisdom,
the unavoidable path
of "learning to be human."

Sometimes for a heart to heal, it must first be broken. What does this mean? Perhaps it means that we must be open, as much as is possible in any given moment, to experiencing the pain as well as the joy of life. If we harden our hearts or create such grand edifices of protection around it so we will never have to experience pain, then we will also never experience the deep, holy joy of true love.

returning to the source

taoist meditation

Allow yourself to become empty.
Abide in stillness.

LAO TZU, *TAO TE CHING (CHAPTER 16)*

IF WE WANT to have a healthy and harmonious relationship with another, we need to also have a healthy and harmonious relationship with ourselves. If we are not centered, not grounded, not trustworthy, then we will not be trusted by another. If we are unhealthy, too self-absorbed, or emotionally unbalanced, then we will not attract a healthy and balanced partner. If we do not know ourselves, we will not be able to know another. And lastly, if we are not developed spiritually, then the challenges of relationship will be too much for us, and we will never be able to achieve sacred union with another.

By practicing meditation, we will become more grounded and emotionally and spiritually balanced. Meditation, both formal and informal, will give us valuable tools to use in stressful times. And because meditation is the practice of connecting to and communing with our higher or spiritual self, it will help us to be more objective in our relationships of all types.

Meditation helps us to calm our mind and our emotions so we do not overreact to every bump in the road. Hua-Ching Ni says in his book *8,000 Years of Wisdom*, "Usually something unimportant stimulates an emotional response, and then one unconsciously emphasizes the trouble to support being emotional."

Taoist meditation is often called "Embracing the One" or "Returning to the Source." There is much about it that is mystical and may at first seem hard to understand for the beginner. It is different from many other forms of Eastern meditation practices because it emphasizes energy practice over mind practice. True, we do use the mind to guide the chi, or internal energy, to quiet the emotions, and to let go of all outside influences—those "external pernicious influences" that stir up the mud of our inner selves. But even when we are sitting still doing nothing *(ching-jing-wu-wei)*, we are still running energy throughout our body or in what is known as the microcosmic orbit (up the back and down the front) or cooking up healing medicine in the cauldron of our lower dan tian.

Most Taoist meditation practice centers on the lower dan tian; however, it is interesting to note that women are often taught to instead put their focus on the middle dan tian, the point between the breasts, just above the solar plexus. This point is connected to the heart center, where the shen resides. It is felt that, because of the superior spiritual nature of women, they do not need to do quite so much of the basic foundational energetic work as men do.

From the outside, the meditating individual appears to be sitting quietly, breathing deeply and gently, with a small half smile on his or her lips. On the inside, however, great forces are at work, reshaping and rerouting streams of energy and light. This internal healing energy then begins reshaping the outside. Not only do regular meditators begin to feel different, they often even *look* different to others. Worry lines and wrinkles begin to relax and disappear; the body, especially the spine, begins to realign itself and the meditator's posture changes. The ability to deal with life's challenges and pressures improves dramatically, and so one's entire disposition changes accordingly.

The internal changes are even more dramatic. A greater sense of clarity, both emotional and psychological, begins to suffuse one's being. As chi pathways begin to unblock and the internal energy of one's body begins to travel more easily and powerfully through one's being, old illnesses and old problems begin to lighten, if not disappear entirely.

Just how does one enter into this state of absolute quiescence, where the chi can do its work? Lao Tzu says:

> Abide in stillness.
> The ten thousand beings rise and flourish
> While the sage watches their return.
> Though all beings exist in profusion
> They all end up returning to their source.
> Returning to their source is called tranquility.
> *(Chapter 16)*

Another traditional name for Taoist meditation is "Abiding in Stillness." Lao Tzu gives us the following advice on stillness practice:

> Go within and retreat from the world.
> Blunt your sharpness,
> separate your entanglements,
> soften your light.
> *(Chapter 56)*

Posture

Most people in the West have a difficult time sitting still. They fidget, stretch, make noises, sway back and forth, changing posture over and over. Yet it is impossible to attain inner stillness without first attaining outer stillness. The very first prerequisite for attaining the deep levels of inner stillness and quietude needed for doing deep meditation work is being able to sit with the spine straight for at least twenty minutes at a time.

Because this is so difficult for many beginners, the best thing to do is start with a small amount of time—say five minutes. After a time, you can extend that period until you can sit for twenty to thirty minutes at a stretch without having to change posture or move around. Twenty or thirty minutes of meditation practice at a time is sufficient for most people. If your goal is to heal a serious health problem or to become an immortal, then much longer periods of sitting will be necessary, but for most people a shorter period will do just fine. Taoists don't really advocate long uninterrupted hours of sitting for most people. Sitting for a long time is said to cause the inner energy to stagnate in the organs and can actually do more harm than good. I was once told by one of my teachers that too much sitting will make your teeth fall out.

You can sit on the floor with your legs crossed or if you can manage it, in the cross-legged position known as half or full lotus. Or else you can sit on the edge of a chair with your feet flat on the floor.

Your hands lie in your lap. You can have the left hand lying in your right palm, with the tips of the thumbs touching. Or you can lay your right thumb in the palm of your left hand, close your left fingers and thumb over it, and wrap your right fingers around your left fist. (This second hand position will look like a yin/yang symbol when you look at the sides of the hands.) You can also lay your hands palms up on your thighs.

It is very important to keep the spine erect and straight, not as if you were standing at attention, but as if there were a string pulling you up from the top of your head, from the bai hui point at the center of the crown; your chin is slightly pulled in, to elongate the neck. This way the energy coming up the du mai channel, which runs up the back of the spine, can flow evenly and smoothly.

It is important not to slump or fidget during the meditation, but it is equally important not to hold yourself too stiffly.

There is no need to be rigid or dogmatic about posture. The idea is to feel balanced and stable. Deep relaxation is imperative, but you don't want to be so relaxed that you topple over to one side or the other; neither do you want to sit too stiffly and end up with a sore back.

Correct relaxation is not collapse. It is an energetic, dynamic type of relaxation in which your muscles, tendons, organs, and nervous system get a chance to refresh and re-energize themselves. Many people, if they allow themselves to totally relax, find themselves falling asleep or nodding out. It is very important to reach a state of dynamic relaxation for meditation or any other type of chi gong practice to be truly effective. There is a great difference between relaxing and going limp.

Watch a cat sometime. Notice how she sits or lies with eyes half-closed or closed, completely relaxed, seemingly deeply asleep. But let a squirrel or bird come anywhere in her vicinity, and she's up like a shot. She has been engaged in a deeply relaxed meditative state yet is able to awaken with no effort and can move with great speed and agility at a moment's notice. That is the type of dynamic relaxation we want to cultivate in Taoist meditation.

Breathing

After mastering sitting still and keeping the spine erect, the next step is breathing correctly. Breathing is something most people feel they can do very well already, but actually, most people don't do a very good job of breathing at all. They breathe mostly from the upper part of the chest and so don't utilize their actual lung power to the fullest.

There is a very large muscle right above our abdominal cavity called the diaphragm, which is shaped like a dome. It can affect the esophagus, the aorta, and the vagus nerve.

When we breathe correctly—from the belly, filling our lungs from the bottom up—we also work that diaphragm muscle, massaging our digestive organs and promoting the flow of blood and lymph to that region. Also, by breathing slowly and deeply, we are better able to arrive at a sense of peacefulness and centeredness. Thus, by simply breathing correctly we can obtain peacefulness and a sense of groundedness and centeredness, as well as promote better digestion and respiration.

Probably the most basic form of breathing in Taoist meditation or other chi gong practices is what is called natural breathing or prenatal breathing. The idea is to breathe into the belly or the lower dan tian as if we were babies breathing in our mother's womb—not through our lungs but through our umbilical cord. When we breathe in, our abdomen expands; when we exhale, our abdomen contracts. All breathing is done through the nose, which is specifically designed to warm and filter the air before it gets to our lungs.

This is a very calming type of breathing. If you practice breathing in this way for even fifteen minutes a day, you will eventually begin breathing this way all of the time, even when you are sleeping, and the benefits will be enormous.

We are all familiar with the "flight or fight" feeling we get when we are alarmed or in shock. What happens to our breath during these times? It pretty much stops or becomes very shallow. If, when we find ourselves in a stressful situation, we pause for a moment to take a few really slow and deep breaths, it can often clear our mind and quiet our nervous system, helping us to better handle the situation.

Extensive literature in the Taoist canon describes various breathing practices, some extremely difficult and requiring the guidance of a teacher. But for basic Taoist meditation practices, such as sitting or even tai chi, the natural breath is sufficient. Practice it daily, and you will be amazed at the sublime effects this simple practice can produce.

Other Details

Have you seen statues of the Buddha, the Awakened One, sitting in meditation? Did you notice the little half smile on his face? He's not sitting there like a lump of wood, solemn and stiff. We need to sit with that same spirit of joy and openness. One of the things I remember most about my first tai chi teacher, David Cheng, was the warm smile he held all through his practice. In Taoism, we believe that it's quite all right to enjoy our practices, that spiritual work can be enjoyable! So relax those facial muscles, and let a small smile play about your lips as you sit. Remember, it takes a lot more muscles to frown than it does to smile.

Energy in the body travels along very specific pathways. Two of the main pathways are the du mai and the ren mai. The du mai runs up the back of the body, and the ren mai runs down the front of the body. The place where they meet is in the upper and lower palate in the mouth. In meditation, as in all chi gong practices, we want to connect those two pathways by placing the tongue lightly upon the upper palate. This connects the two pathways, much like completing an electrical circuit. When these pathways are linked, the chi can circulate in an efficient manner.

Placing the tongue on the palate also produces greater amounts of saliva. Taoists believe saliva is a precious substance, and it is often called such fanciful names as "golden dew." Saliva contains proteins, hormones, and other substances that have digestive and antibacterial functions. It is not a nasty waste product, but a vital, healthful substance that we can use for our own benefit.

It is believed that correct breathing fills our saliva with chi, which we can then swallow down into our internal organs. Whenever we have accumulated a good amount of saliva, we should swallow it forcefully, imagining that it is traveling all the way into our lower dan tian, our field of elixir. There are certain practices where you roll the tongue around the inside of the mouth in order to accumulate a good amount of saliva and then separate the mouthful of saliva into three parts and swallow them each separately, sometimes moving them down to each side of the abdomen and then to the center.

Many people find that closing their eyes helps them shut out extraneous distraction from the outside world. The danger is that you may be tempted to zone out or even fall asleep. Taoist meditation is not about going into a trance or falling asleep. Instead, it is a form of dynamic interaction between our outer and inner selves. If closing your eyes leads to less internal focus rather than more, instead keep them in a half-closed position and let your gaze become unfocused.

✤ Healing Meditation

Sit in a comfortable position on a cushion or chair, or lie comfortably on the floor or a bed. Relax completely, from the top of your head to the bottoms of your feet. Feel each part of your body relax as you slowly pan your attention down your head, face, neck, shoulders, upper chest, upper arms, lower arms, hands, fingers, abdomen, groin, thighs, upper legs, knees, lower legs, feet, and toes.

Breathe slowly and deeply through your nose, the tip of your tongue resting on the top palate of your mouth. As you breathe in, breathe in bright light or healing chi. Let it fill your entire body, going deep within your body and psyche, flowing into all the dark and pain-filled areas of your body and psyche. As you breathe out, allow all the pain, sickness, or stress to leave your body, like a dark smoke or mist. With your inner eye, watch that mist fade off into the air.

Keep breathing slowly and deeply. Keep allowing your body to fill with healing, relaxing light and let all the pain, disease, sorrow, and stress leave you. Do this for ten to twenty minutes—or longer, if need be.

When you feel done, rub your palms together thirty-six times and then rub your hands up and down your face at least three times. Then open your eyes and re-enter the world around you, renewed and relaxed.

You can do this meditation whenever you feel the need to recharge or detoxify your system, though if you do it at night, be sure to direct the energy to your lower abdomen and not into your head when you finish, or you may have trouble sleeping.

The Mind

Many people find it very difficult to enter a deep state of meditation because their mind is so full of thoughts, which lead to other thoughts, which lead to others, and so on and on. It can be helpful to count your breaths from one to ten, concentrating fully on each count. Then, once you reach ten, go back and start over again. In the beginning it is often difficult to count much past ten without the thoughts starting up again, but with time, it will become easier. In fact, it is just about impossible to completely still the mind. But even a few moments of deep meditation can have great effects on your mind-body system.

Unlike some other forms of meditation, which are solely for the purpose of quieting the mind, Taoist meditation seeks to quiet the mind so that it will be out of the way and the chi can move in its own fashion. Taoist meditation masters created moving meditation forms, such as tai chi, that allow people to move in a slow and flowing meditative state, which, in turn, allows the chi in their bodies to move on its own. Tai chi is often called "stillness within movement." In still sitting, there is a "movement within stillness."

This inner movement is the healing, vitalizing chi moving deep within the three dan tians, opening energy pathways as well as spiritual centers. It is also how we find our deep connection with the eternal. The more we dwell within that state in meditation, the easier it is for it to carry over into the rest of our lives.

All Taoist practices are about refining our energy, our chi, and our spirit, or shen. This refinement process has many levels—psychological, emotional, and spiritual. It is also concerned with the internal process of refining our jing, or fundamental energy, into chi, then refining that into pure spiritual energy, or shen, and then transforming that back into Tao. It is a slow process, taking many years of serious practice to fully accomplish. But there are many helpful results that occur along the way, making the practice itself a rewarding and educational process.

In Taoist practice it is said that "chi follows yi," or chi follows the mind. It is an ancient and well-known fact that we can lead energy in our body with our minds. There is even a relatively new branch of Western medicine called psychoneuroimmunology, which means basically the same thing. For example, patients with tumors are taught to send little white knights or *Pac-Man*-type creatures to defeat or eat up the rampaging cancer cells in their body, often to great effect.

৶ Stillness Practice

If we allow ourselves to be knocked off our emotional or psychological center too easily, we will have a difficult time adjusting to the ups and downs that happen even in the most harmonious relationships. This practice can help us find our still center in the midst of activity. Then if in our relationship life we are knocked off our center, we have a way to find it again.

First, sit on a cushion high enough and firm enough to support your lower back, or sit on the front part of a chair with your feet planted firmly on the floor. It is extremely important to keep your spine erect yet not stiff. Never slump on your cushion or chair.

Next, bounce around for a moment, letting the unprocessed energy of the day settle down in your body. Then exhale deeply and suddenly, emptying your lungs fully. Take three deep breaths, then either close your eyes or keep them unfocused in a half-closed position. Relax your shoulders, and begin to breathe deeply and slowly, from the belly. Place the tip of your tongue on your upper palate, and relax your face into a small smile.

Place your mind, or your attention, on your lower dan tian, in your lower abdomen. Allow yourself to feel your breath, your chi, flowing into your dan tian and then back out again in a slow, rhythmic way. Feel yourself fill up with good, clean, healing chi and then feel yourself exhale all the old, unclean, used up chi. Just relax and let this rhythmic exchange happen by itself. Have no effort, no tension, no desire, no agenda, no goal. Just let yourself be carried on the wings of energy and of Tao itself. Let yourself sink deeply into the still, quiet depths of your own being.

You may experience important insights or ideas at this time. It is fine to have a piece of paper and a pen handy to briefly write them down, but then continue with the stillness practice.

When your time is up or you feel that your sense of inner quietude is beginning to dissolve, bring your palms in front of you and rub them together briskly thirty-six times. Place them over your eyes, inhaling the warmth of your palms deep into your eyes and brain. Then rub them gently or briskly up and down over your face three times.

When you are finished, sit for a moment or so with your palms placed over your lower dan tian, below your navel. Let the warmth of your palms enter your dan tian and store up the good warm, healing chi there.

Coming out of Meditation

Be careful how you re-enter the world after deep meditation. Try not to jump right into your workaday world immediately. Take at least three to five minutes to gather your energy. If you can, sit down and drink a cup of tea, or do some gentle stretching. Avoid talking with other people too soon. You will be in a heightened and extremely sensitive state at this time; if you plunge too quickly into your everyday life or if you encounter a tense situation or energy exchange with someone else, you will feel it very deeply and be easily knocked off balance. So take it easy with yourself, like the cat who stretches fully and yawns deeply a few times before slowly entering the outer world on her own terms.

Seeing Within

Taoist meditation is designed for building vital energy and then circulating that within the body. Much of what we know today as the meridian system, which is used in Chinese medicine and chi gong practice, was mapped by those inner astronauts, the ancient Taoists, who while sitting in deep meditation, were able to track how and where energy moved in their bodies. When I was a kid, I had a model called the Visible Man; it was a human body with clear skin, which enabled me to see all the inner organs. The ancient Taoists had their own form of Visible Man because they were able to open, with their inner vision, windows into their own bodies and see how they worked, all without the aid of dissection.

Lao Tzu says that:

> Without going out your door,
> you may know everything under heaven.
> Without looking out the window,
> you can see the Tao of heaven.
> (Chapter 47)

Using our inner vision, we are better able to see our true path in life, to travel through the wilds of our emotional landscape, and to traverse the deep rivers and ravines of our inner being and arrive back home, back at our eternal source, back at Tao.

We can also utilize the power of quietude and stillness in Taoist meditation to hear the inspiration and guidance of our higher self or our guardian or helping spirits. Taoists, like Native Americans and many other peoples, believe that we are surrounded by helpful spirit guides at all times, though these spirits are very hard to hear above the usual symphony of noise that plays in our heads most of the time. We need to become quiet inside in order to hear the "still, small voice within" and benefit from the guidance we receive.

⚜ Under Golden Pond Meditation

Tao may be likened to a great pool of still water, deep, dark, and eternally calm. It is in this great pool that each one of us is born, lives out our lives, and returns to after death. In truth, we never leave it.

Picture yourself, then, as a little frog, sitting quietly on a lily pad, which floats gently on the surface of this pond. It is a bright, hot day, and the sounds of the world are loud and cacophonous. Planes fly overhead, cars whoosh by, children play, and adults argue around your pond.

After listening to the barrage of noise for long enough, you gently plop yourself over the edge of the lily pad and allow yourself to sink into the depths of the pond.

Down and down you go, effortlessly sinking ever deeper into the warm, dark depth of the pond. Down through the layers you go, past darting fish and lumbering turtles. Past the gracefully waving arms of underwater plants you go, like a little weighted doll, until at last you sink to the bottom.

At first it is very muddy, as your presence churns up the silt and sediment on the bottom of the pond. You can't really see anything, and outer sounds are indistinct. You can only sit, listening to the quiet thump of your heart. The rush of the world is far above you now and doesn't affect you anymore. You feel the smooth current of the water dancing all around you.

Then slowly, as the silt and mud sink back down to the bottom and the water gradually clears, you can, perhaps for the first time, see clearly everything surrounding you. The water is warm and soothing. You sit very still, enveloped in this great soothing, motherly world of water. You breathe slowly and deeply, drawing the healing water into your belly. Your breath slows down until you yourself are breathed, the rhythm of breath itself taking over. Your heartbeat slows down also, matching your breath, matching the rhythm of nature, of Tao.

All worldly cares slip away as you are enfolded into a vast and limitless world where you as an individual are no longer important. The small self you have clung to all your life recedes into a much grander sense of Self, of connection to something larger and more eternal. The little pond you sit in expands outward to become a great sea of chi, of life. You sit here, suspended effortlessly, eternally present in an eternal moment of clarity and wisdom.

After a time, you release a little bubble of chi into the water and begin your ascent back into the world. You float up slowly through the water all the way back to the surface, where you jump back onto your lily pad, renewed, refreshed, and ready to begin your life again.

"Why is this important?" you may ask. What does meditation have to do with sex and relationship? The answer is that if you cannot find the stillness within your being, you will not be able to connect in a deep way with another. If you are not in touch with the deepest part of you, how can you hope to understand the deepest part of someone else?

It is by meditation, contemplation, exploration, and the willingness to delve deeply into your own psyche and inner knowing that you will find the wisdom and clarity to go forth into the world of sacred union. As Chuang Tzu reminds us, "We cannot see our reflection in running water, but only in still water. Only a person who has attained inner stillness is able to still the minds of others."

9

the watercourse way

Under heaven there is nothing more yielding
and soft than water.
Yet for attacking what is hard and stiff
there is nothing better.

LAO TZU, *TAO TE CHING (CHAPTER 78)*

THE IMAGE OF water is used over and over again in Taoism to denote the qualities of humbleness, flexibility, adaptability, persistence, and acceptance. Indeed, Tao itself is likened to water by Lao Tzu:

> The highest sage is like water.
> Water benefits the ten thousand beings
> yet contends with no one.
> It flows in places that people reject.
> In this way it is close to Tao.
> *(Chapter 8)*

Taoism uses the image of water to emphasize the soft overcoming the hard. Water can overcome obstacles, not only by going around them, but also by simply biding its time and slowly eroding the obstacle, bit by tiny bit, until eventually a canyon is formed. This is a central tenet of Taoist philosophy: we can meet obstacles in our lives and find ways to creatively and constructively deal with them. The idea is not to avoid or run away from them or, on the other hand, try to ram head on into them. Instead, by going slowly and assuming the quality of water, we can, perhaps, find a way to flow around, over, or under them. Like water, we must be patient enough to realize that in time things will change because that is the nature of all things. *The only constant is change.*

So it is in life, and so it is in love and relationships. The qualities of water—patience, perseverance, flexibility, humbleness, ability to meet obstacles without fear—are as essential to relationships as they are to life in general.

Sometimes We're Up, Sometimes We're Down

Hua-Ching Ni wrote this beautiful passage in his book *The Gentle Path of Spiritual Progress:*

> Sometimes you do better in life, and other times you do poorly. When your cycle is high, you enjoy your life more than when you are having difficulties in a low cycle. To harmonize the flow of your life, don't become excited by the high points or depressed by the low. Always remember the high is built by the low. You should respect the times when you are in a low cycle . . . When people have a low cycle, they think of it in an emotional way and feel terrible. They want to die or kill themselves. They feel boring, unattractive, and uninteresting . . . They don't realize that their low cycle can make them wise. Life is built up by each uninteresting moment, not just by excitement. *(Chapter 26)*

To the Taoist, exalting the high in place of the low is to lose sight of the truth of how things really are. Our lives are filled with endless moments when nothing seems to be happening, when we seem to be stuck in a rut or making no progress at all. According to the Taoists, it is in these moments, these dull and uninteresting moments, that we can be building the foundation to sagehood. As Hua-Ching Ni says, "Life is built up by each uninteresting moment."

All life is cycles, say the Taoists. Some days we are up, other days we are down. Relationships also go through similar cycles. This is important to remember. We must not allow ourselves to get too bent out of shape every time we, our partner, or our relationship itself go into a low cycle. This can take the shape of an emotional, energetic, or even physical low cycle. These periods can be an opportunity to talk to each other about what is going on. Or it can be a chance to look at ourselves more deeply and see how our own behavior or attitude is contributing to the problem. Then again, sometimes there is just no way to know what is causing the low cycle, and all we can do is ride it out and be especially kind and patient with each other and ourselves.

Taoists respect low cycles as opportunities for growth. Most of us hate being in a low cycle and generally wish to get out of it as soon as possible. But sometimes just allowing ourselves to be there with it, for as long as it takes to turn around, is the best thing we can do. It is not always possible to understand why our relationship cycle is low, which can be very frustrating. Taoist teachers say this is not the time to be hitting our heads against the wall and trying to force a change but is the time to relax and slowly build up our energy. This way, when the cycle shifts again, as it always does, we will be ready for it.

A stream can rush merrily along only until it comes up against some sort of dam in the flow. Perhaps a log has fallen into the water and is plugging it up. The water can try to go under the log, but if the log is lying on the floor of the stream, it cannot. It may try to go around the wood, but if the log is also lying across the whole width of the stream, it cannot do that either. The water seems to be blocked and stopped in its tracks. But in a little while, the water that has continued to flow downstream will raise the level of the stream until it can pour over the obstruction and go on its way.

Often we may feel like we are stuck, that there is nothing happening with our lives or our relationship. We want to force our way past the log that is blocking our progress. Sometimes we are successful, and sometimes we are not. But if we just relax, say the Taoists, and allow our inner energy to slowly rise of its own accord, we may find ourselves sailing along again, at an even greater speed and depth than before.

Flexibility Is a Must

It is when we act without flexibility that we lose the sacred thread of our relationship and get bogged down in what we *want* to have happen instead of what *is* happening. Lao Tzu talks about the young plant that is green, juicy, and supple and can bend with the wind and not break. He then goes on to describe the old plant, which is dry and brittle and easily breaks.

> When we are born, we are supple and tender,
> like a young plant.
> When we die, we become rigid and unyielding.
> The ten thousand beings,
> including plants and grasses,
> when they are young are soft and pliable.
> At their death, they are dry and brittle.
> Therefore, we say that the stiff and unyielding
> are the companions of death.
> The soft and yielding are the followers of life.
> In this way, an army may be strong,
> but it will be defeated.
> A mighty tree will be cut down.
> The great and mighty will fall,
> while the soft and yielding will overcome.
> (Chapter 76)

So too can we, as humans, become more brittle and less flexible as we age. Instead of moving gracefully through the world and our lives, we often get stuck in unhealthy lifestyles—eating unhealthy foods, watching too much television, not moving our bodies enough, or abusing ourselves with drugs such as coffee, sugar, cigarettes, and other, more illicit drugs. No matter what our unhealthy habits are, they harm our chi, which disturbs our inner harmony and affects our emotional life greatly. Remember, emotions are a type of energy. What we do with our body affects our emotions in a big way.

We can become brittle and inflexible on the inside as well. We stop learning new things and experiencing new ideas, new thoughts, new sights, new sounds. We get set in our ways and forget how exciting and fun and truly amazing life can be—if we only open ourselves to it, if we only "let the sunshine in."

Lao Tzu asks if we can become supple and relaxed as a child. Chuang Tzu describes how babies can cry at the top of their lungs for hours at a time and not get tired or lose their voice. Master Jesus said that we must become as children to enter the kingdom of heaven.

What all these sages are talking about is the ability to experience life with all the freshness and nonresistance of a child. It is not about being child*ish*, which many adults are good at, but being child*like*—being able to laugh at life's absurdities, being able to play, being open to new experiences.

Maintaining a childlike demeanor within a relationship also means bringing joy and laughter into it, as well as helping us maintain our flexibility. Movies show us, over and over again, the wild passion of lovers ripping each other's clothes off in a feverish rush toward sex. Then they show the lovers after sex, smoking or sleeping or perhaps talking. What they never show is lovers laughing together in bed! Laughing together is very important and a sign of a healthy sex life. We need to be able to laugh at ourselves and in all kinds of situations, including sex. Playing together, laughing together, exploring new things and experiences together—these are some of the very best ways to keep a relationship alive and healthy and in a continually growing and evolving state.

The Dance of Partnership

If we cannot laugh at ourselves and each other, we tend to fall into a dull rut of a relationship. It is important, in sacred union, to find a *groove*, not a rut. There is a difference. Finding a good groove is like dancing together. Both of you are finding a way to be with the music of your life together. First one person leads, then the other. You both feel the connection, the sacred thread of your communion, and you are both excited and charged about it. You feel yourselves filled up with the music of your life and are able to move gracefully and effortlessly with it.

This is not to say that, in your dance together, you will never step on each other's feet. It means recognizing that when your partner steps on your foot, he or she did so unintentionally and not out of malice. And the more conscious you both are about your dance together, the less likely this will happen.

Sometimes in the dance of partnership, we take the lead and want to keep it. We all have our favorite ways we like things to be. We all have ideas or agendas of what we would like to see happening with our relationships, especially at the beginning of new relationship. We all want to shape situations to our own specifications in order to be happy. We all want things to go right for us as much as possible. But being too attached to our agendas will only stop the flow of chi and love and bind up the sacred thread of our love life. If we are truly interested in getting to know someone better or getting closer and more intimate with someone, we cannot force our agenda on them. We have to be flexible enough to find a balance between what is comfortable for them and what is comfortable for us.

The Watercourse Way in the Bedroom

Being flexible and honoring our partner's desires as much as our own is especially important with sexuality. I came up in the sixties generation, when people fell into bed with each other at the drop of a hat, without taking any time to get to know each other at all. Some people still do this today. But if we want our sexual relationship to be as deep and sacred as it can be, we have to be willing to go slowly and find a common ground of trust and intimacy.

Men, being of the fire element, which blazes up so easily and quickly, have a harder time slowing down than women, who are the water element, which takes time to boil. Some people can find a place of intimacy and harmony very quickly, but many people take longer to feel that sense of trust and depth of communion that they need before they are ready to open sexually to another.

If the man is too pushy and demanding, if he cannot wait until the woman is ready to flower in her own time, then he will lose the precious gift of that flowering. If he tries to force the woman to move at his pace, before she is ready to, then it will only cause more wounding and create more disharmony between them. And after all, what is the rush? Anything really good is worth waiting for. If she is not really open in her flowering, sex will not be a sacred act but merely a physical one, devoid of anything holy and healing.

As discussed in chapter 3, slowing down and matching each other's pace is important, both in deciding when to have sex and in the act of sex itself. Say a man is interested in having sex with his partner one night. He is feeling all juiced up and ready to go. His fiery nature allows him to reach this place very quickly and effortlessly. The woman, on the other hand, is of a watery nature and needs to arrive in that place much more slowly and in different ways than the man. If the man slows his fire down enough to match the woman, then they can move together into a mutual place of juicy, sexual energy. But if the man tries to move things along too quickly, without giving the woman time to match his energy or without slowing his own energy down to match hers, there will be no meeting. Chances are either they will not have sex or, if they do, the woman will just be giving in to the man's energy, and there will be no deep heart connection.

In *Harmony: The Art of Life*, Hua-Ching Ni says, "There is no benefit in sex without love because your soul is not kindled."

If occasionally the woman just cannot meet the man in the sexual arena, the man must be able to relax, let go of his desire for sex, and be okay with what is. This can be very difficult for many men. But if he remembers to connect with the Watercourse Way, he will be better able to not only be okay with whatever energy there is between him and his partner but also will harbor no ill will and will not be filled with disappointment and frustration.

Remember, to Taoists, sexual energy is primarily creative, expansive energy that can be used for other things besides the sexual act itself. Taoist practices are full of ways to sublimate or direct energy—sexual or otherwise—for greater health and benefit. The Taoist seeks to make food or medicine out of everything that happens to him or her—emotional challenges, including relationship challenges; physical challenges, including sexual challenges; and challenges to the spirit.

Just like the stream that picks up many kinds of water and other things like leaves, limbs, and even whole trees, as it travels to the river and then to the sea, so do we, as moving water, take on many different experiences in our lives, in our own journey to the sea, or Tao. If we can emulate those qualities of water—the ability to go with the flow, to take whatever shape it finds itself in, to be flexible, graceful, and undemanding—we will succeed in our quest for sacred union.

৬❀ Water Meditation

Here is a little meditation and visualization that will help you connect more deeply to the Watercourse Way.

Imagine yourself lying on the ground on the edge of a fast-running stream. Hear the sound of the gurgling water as it runs past your head. Allow the sound to fill your entire being.

After a few moments, feel yourself slip into the water. As you are carried along in the swiftly moving stream, feel your own sense of self melt into the water until, instead of being carried along by the water, you are the water itself.

Feel yourself rushing downstream, flowing effortlessly over rocks and sand, flowing down toward the sea. Explore what it feels like to be water, to flow along so swiftly and effortlessly. Feel yourself flow up and over any rock or tree branch that gets in your way.

After a time, feel your water body become larger and deeper as the stream enters the river. Here the current may slow down as the stream becomes the river. Feel yourself embracing all the flotsam and jetsam that pours into the river, pulled along by the strong current. Rather than complaining or feeling frustrated or attacked by these obstructions, you are able to assimilate them into your flow and carry them along with you.

During this time, feel your water self flowing along, being fed by many other swiftly moving streams. Feel your being expand and become wider and deeper, moving always downhill, toward the sea. As flowing water, you have no agenda except to join yourself with the great ocean of existence, or what might be called Tao. And once you reach your goal, you pour yourself into it unreservedly, joyously.

Then the sun comes out and draws you up toward the sky, where you join the clouds that move slowly over the earth and eventually open and drop you back upon the earth, where you can once again become a stream moving down toward the sea.

As with all Taoist meditation practices, come out of this one slowly. Rub your hands together thirty-six times and then up and down your face before you open your eyes.

10

love and marriage

The best situation is when a couple can complement each
other's personalities, abilities, strengths, and weaknesses.

HUA-CHING NI, *MOONLIGHT IN THE DARK NIGHT*

TRADITIONAL TAOIST TEXTS don't have a lot to say about love
and marriage. (Throughout this chapter, please feel free to substitute
the word *relationship* for *marriage,* if you like.) You won't find stories
about star-crossed lovers or directions on how to find the perfect mate.
However, the basic Taoist principles of yin/yang, of how to conduct
oneself in relationship with others, of how to use whatever situation we
find ourselves in as a form of self-cultivation, can all be applied to the
subject of love and marriage.

Many people end up in relationships out of fear—fear of being alone,
fear of being unloved, fear of being left behind, fear of growing old or of
dying without company. But is fear the right thing to base a marriage on?

Many people view love as some sort of uncontainable, uncontrollable force of energy that explodes on contact. But to base a marriage
on anything other than true heart love, respect, and mutual cooperation is to invite disaster.

Many people view their emotional ties through the lens of their
moods or whims. When they are in one mood, their partner is the

most wonderful person on the earth. Then, when they are not feeling so good, the other person is suddenly their worst enemy. In an ancient text called the *Han Fei Tzu,* we find the following story:

> In ancient China there lived a beautiful woman named Mi Tzu-hsia, who was the favorite of the Lord of Wei. At that time, according to the law, anyone found riding in the lord's carriage without his permission was punished by having their foot cut off. Once, when Mi Tzu-hsia's mother became ill, she was so upset that she immediately set out in the lord's carriage to see her without consulting the lord. But when the lord found out, he only praised her for her filial devotion. "Imagine," he said, "risking such a severe punishment for her mother!"
>
> One day while she and her lord were walking in the garden, Mi Tzu-hsia picked a ripe peach and, finding it so delicious, she gave it to her lord to finish. Again he praised her, saying how much she must love him to forget her own pleasure to share it with him.
>
> But years later, as Mi Tzu-hsia's beauty began to fade, she fell out of favor with her lord. Then one day, when she had done something to offend him, he rebuked her saying, "I remember how she once took my carriage without my permission. And another time she gave me a peach that she had already bitten into!" *(Tales from the Tao, chapter 33)*

Beauty will fade with age, health will decline, wealth can be lost, celebrity will go out of fashion. When choosing a life partner, it is best not to base your decision on superficial things. Make your decision, rather, with the intelligence of the heart.

True Love

For millennia now, we humans have been trying to understand this strange attraction called love. How do we know when love is real? Can we still love that person even when we are angry with them? Can we still love them even though we cannot become accustomed to their bad habits? Can we still love them even when they no longer surprise us?

The old saying that you must learn to love yourself before you can love another is true. Indeed, we can never even know another before we know ourselves. And we can certainly never understand another before we begin to have some understanding of ourselves.

When true love blooms, it does so not only in our heart, but in our very soul. True love, like Tao itself, cannot be put into words. It can be alluded to but never really captured. It can be described but never really explained. Sometimes the only way we can truly know love is by its absence. Or perhaps love is a certain indefinable something that makes us feel better about ourselves when we are with a person, something that calls out to us from the deepest part of our being.

Love can bring out the best in us. Interestingly enough, it can also bring out the worst in us. It can take us to the greatest heights of ecstasy, or it can break our hearts and make us wish we had never been born. It can inspire us or destroy us. It can heal us or break us. It can give us joy, passion, contentment, and a reason to live. It can also cause sadness, misery, and unfulfilled desire and make us want to die. Yet when we say yes to love, we are saying yes to life itself. And to say no to love is to say no to life. To close our hearts to love is to cut ourselves off from the very source of all life. To be afraid of love is to fear our very soul's most secret desire.

Love can often conquer all mortal boundaries. When someone we love passes on, do we forget them? Do they not still live in our hearts and minds?

True Marriage

Marriage is another subject that has mystified and confused people for many generations. What is a good marriage? How can we make marriage last? How do we know the other person is the right one for us? How do we deal with problems when they arise?

A marriage could be seen as two countries, existing side-by-side, with interconnecting borders and a common, or at least similar, language. There are sometimes feuds, misunderstandings, even boycotts. But as long as these don't escalate to outright war, the marriage can work.

We must ask ourselves, what is the marriage for? Is it enabling two people to avoid loneliness? Is it for two people so in love with each other they can't bear to be apart? Is it to produce children and create a family? Is it to form a partnership of the heart and soul?

It may be said that in marriage we can find all the challenges and opportunities we need for self-cultivation. When we look at marriage as an opportunity for us to work toward self-realization, we will see it in a different light than merely two people living together because they have signed a piece of paper that gives them permission to marry.

Taoists use *everything* in their life for their self-cultivation. This includes their relationships, their health issues, their work, their suffering, and their joy. If we view marriage as a spiritual agreement between two souls, we can be better equipped to weather the emotional storms that come up in every relationship.

Letting Go

Taoists teach that it is our spiritual self that should be running our life instead of our intellectual mind, as it is in most people. The mind should be the servant of our spirit instead of our spirit being the slave of our mind. Our spirit is boundless and depthless. Our mind is conditioned by its experience in the world, from childhood on, and by the mores and cultural ideas that surround us. Lao Tzu says that in the world of the mind, each day something new is taken on. But in the world of the spirit, the world of Tao, each day something is let go of.

Conflict within a relationship provides many opportunities for letting go of something that doesn't serve us. For instance, by letting go of the need to dominate or defend ourselves against our partner, both sides can begin to breathe and move freely within the relationship. When a relationship devolves into constant sniping, it often means that one person is feeling powerless, and the only way they can make themselves feel better is to harp on the other person's failures or inconsistencies. Often when we are complaining about something in our partner, it is because we know, deep down inside, that we are really complaining about ourselves. We feel we are not able to measure up to a highly idealized version of relationship; we feel as though we are constantly failing to meet the high standards that we are holding ourselves and our partner to.

In the world of the Tao of intimacy and ecstasy, we instead try our best to let go of such unnatural standards and instead embrace who we and our partner really are, in all our beautiful glory and flawed beauty. We have faith that our partner is doing his or her best in any one situation, just as we are. If we allow ourselves to believe that most people are, in fact, doing the best they can most of the time, we can perhaps let go of some of our resentment toward them for not always pleasing us. If we can liberate ourselves and our partner from always having to do the right thing, we can then begin to really get to know ourselves and each other. If we can let go of unrealistic concepts about love, marriage, and how our partner should be, perhaps we will learn to love in a much deeper, wider, and more open way.

Conflict also invites us to let go of the need to defend ourselves and to drop the need to always be right. Sometimes during conflict, the most loving thing to do, both for ourselves and our partner, is to experience being totally and completely wrong, yet not feeling guilty about it or feeling the need to make a lot of excuses. We can just drop our defensiveness and say, "I was wrong about that," or my favorite,

"Credit me with an error." Sometimes we are just wrong. There is just no getting around it. If we feel that admitting it will give our partner some sort of power over us, we will be cut off from fully embracing disgrace willingly. Our partner could be giving us a way to release ourselves from the tyranny of always needing to be right! When we can learn to own our side of whatever conflict has arisen, without shame and guilt, then we can relax into our own true being and expand our ability to love, deeply and fully.

Lao Tzu describes the sage person this way:

> She is not aggressive,
> and so she is able to achieve greatness.
> She does not boast,
> and so she is recognized by all.
> She does not contend,
> and so no one under heaven
> contends with her.
> *(Chapter 22)*

Letting go of our defensiveness, our need to be right, our need to win the battle, does not mean that we need to submit to someone else's attempt to control us, make us wrong, shame us, or abuse us. Attempting to have power over our partner is certainly not the Tao of intimacy and ecstasy.

If only one person in the relationship takes these practices to heart and the other one does not, it will be very difficult, if not impossible, to reach a level of true sacred union. Sacred union is a dance that needs both partners to be willing to come out onto the dance floor and find a way to move together. Sometimes the dance may be graceful; sometimes it may be awkward. But both partners need to be interested in and committed to dancing in harmony, or else it cannot work.

The Spiritual Marriage

What is a spiritual marriage? It can be anything from a relationship in which the couple pray or worship together to one in which each individual recognizes and respects the other's natural divinity. It is not necessary to have the support or recognition of an organized religion to feel that you are in a spiritual marriage. That is between both of you and your own natural spiritual nature.

By creating bonds that reach beyond this material life, we can create a true and eternal marriage "made in heaven." A marriage based, at least in part, on spiritual agreement will continue to grow and flourish long after you have both gotten to know each other in excruciating detail. A marriage based on a spiritual foundation will provide inspiration and instruction long after the initial excitement has worn off.

A spiritual marriage is one of balance between yin and yang. For many centuries, in China, the prevailing cultural norm regarding love and marriage was Confucianism. This was a philosophy of order that put the emperor at the very apex of society, which then descended in importance through the court officials, and in each household, through the father and then through the sons. Women ranked after the sons in importance. Under Confucianism, women, with their mutilated feet, were housebound, uneducated, and had no voice in politics, society, or any aspect of life outside their tightly bound world.

One famous Confucian work, called the *Nu-Chieh (The Ideal Woman)* tells us that a girl baby, in order to establish her subservience in life, should be immediately hidden under the bed. Then the parents are told to fast for three days and offer prayers to the ancestral gods for having made the mistake of having a girl child. When grown, the woman's role in life was to serve the males in her family (husband and sons), and her highest virtues were modesty and obedience. She was taught to walk backward from any room in which there were men present and to always regard herself as being wrong in any dispute.

How far these teachings differed from those of Lao Tzu and Chuang Tzu, who respected and even venerated the superiority of the yin over the yang. With their emphasis on the yin, the essentially maternal, feminine energy of the universe, Taoists have always supported women's rights and privileges, even as Chinese culture became dominated by the inherently antifeminine Confucians and then by the puritanical Communists. Know the yang, but hold to the yin, says Lao Tzu. Know the important creative power of the yang, but do not let go of the enormously creative power of the yin—the dark, mysterious, watery womb of our origin.

It is only when this balance is maintained that it is possible for men and women to come together in any sort of equality and harmony. It is in using the many energetic, emotional, and sexual practices of the path of Tao that men and women can create and sustain long-term healthy relationships. And while it may be hard to find in Taoist texts references to what we may think of as romantic love as in the West, Taoism still gives us many guidelines and teachings that may be useful in today's often confusing world of love and relationship.

For example, the traditional Chinese thought women were inherently more spiritual than men, and therefore, it was easier for them to attain Tao. Also, women, because of their ability to give birth, were considered more powerful than men.

A balance of yin and yang, of both aggressive and supportive energies, is needed for a successful and spiritual relationship. It is only when men and women can come together with equal and mutual respect that a deep and long-term relationship, a sacred union, is possible. Even in same-sex relationships there is always still an exchange of yin and yang energies, and a balance of yin and yang is still necessary. By being respectful of the roles yin and yang play in a relationship and by paying close attention to the balance and harmony of each other's energetic and emotional states, you can build a strong and lasting relationship. By being aware of and sensitive to the balance and subtle shifts of our own yin and yang qualities, as well as internal energetic ebbs and flows, we are better able to make proper decisions and conduct ourselves with integrity and foresight in our dealings with others.

For a spiritual marriage, we want to create bonds beyond this material life, yet at the same time, that marriage or partnership must be grounded in reality. And it is simply not realistic for one person to fill every possible need of the other.

In ancient times and in many different cultures, both ancient and modern, marriages were arranged. The idea of falling in love with someone first and then marrying them was very foreign to most people. Marriage was seen as providing a partner to produce children and to help with the labor of growing food or maintaining a business or craft. If love followed marriage, all well and good, but love was not necessarily expected.

Nowadays people have all sorts of often-unrealistic expectations of their partners. In order to stay monogamous, we tend to expect our partners to be all things, from seducer to supporter. It is the inability of any one person to fulfill this role for another that can lead to much dissatisfaction and unhappiness.

Anyone seeking perfection in another person will be disappointed. Anyone seeking perfection in a relationship will be discontented. Having realistic expectations and desires will allow each person in the relationship, and the relationship itself, to grow and thrive in a natural fashion.

Sustaining the Spiritual Marriage

In the Taoist concept of leading from behind, we see one way of creating a mutually satisfying and workable marriage or relationship. One does not always have to be in the leadership position to achieve satisfaction. A mutual exchange and sharing of ideas, thoughts, and feelings is the best way to build a relationship.

Marriage, like spiritual cultivation, happens little by little, during many small, unexciting moments. Unlike the movies, where everything happens in grand fashion, with swelling music and teary-eyed close-ups, real life can be dull and simple. It is in the constant flow of the simple and commonplace that real growth takes place. By giving each other permission to make mistakes, to learn about ourselves in real time, to go through periods of confusion and doubt, we will actually strengthen the roots of our relationship, so it can grow and flourish as a true spiritual marriage.

When we are in the midst of an intense emotional state, we do not always think, speak, or act correctly. We often say or do things that we regret later. We must be willing to forgive ourselves for these times, and at the same time, we must be able to forgive our partner if, in the heat of an argument, they say or do things that they later regret.

When you find yourself in an intense emotional state, stop, and breathe deeply from the belly. Take a moment to compose your thoughts and to let your true feelings come through.

If you find yourself having the same negative emotions over and over again, instead of blaming your partner, look at yourself and see where these feelings could be coming from. Remember, oftentimes emotions can be caused by energetic or physiological imbalances and can be treated as such.

To be successful in relationship, one must give up one's idea of a perfect relationship. To be happy in relationship, one must learn how to be happy without a relationship.

Taoists say that if one desires to receive, they must first give, and you cannot give what you don't yourself have. To get what you want out of a relationship, you must first learn how to give that same thing to another. To make a marriage last, both people must grow, both individually and together. A marriage based on mutual interests and a spiritual understanding, even if you are on different paths, will outlast a marriage based on mutual needs and unrealistic expectations. On the other hand, if there is no harmony between you, the marriage cannot last. Or if it does, it will be a prison for you both.

It is by going deep within ourselves that we find a sense of what it is that we seek in another. It is also important for us to learn how to give ourselves what we need. We cannot wait until someone comes along to complete us, to give our lives form and substance. That is something that we need to do for ourselves. Then, when someone does come along, they will find a whole, harmonized being waiting for them!

In times of great stress, it is important not to burden each other overmuch with doubts and demands. By seeking support outside the relationship from friends and family or even professionally, you will be better able to weather the difficult times.

Another important aspect of sustaining relationship is letting each other remain individuals. While it may be nice at first to completely merge personalities and energy fields, in the long run it will be better to come together as two separate and clearly defined individuals. It is important not to lose sight of your own individuality when in a serious relationship. Losing your own identity in another will create problems in the long run.

Again, it is not necessary that you both be on the identical spiritual path or follow the same religion, but if there is some sort of spiritual base in your relationship, it will be much easier to deal successfully with the challenges every marriage faces. Look to your own spiritual cultivation and allow your partner to look to theirs. In this way, you will both meet in the center and benefit from each other's cultivation.

In any long-term relationship things will change, people will change, circumstances will change. When one person in the marriage is ready for change or growth but the other is not, the marriage seldom survives. If you are able to flow along with the other person's changes, like water flowing though different pathways, the relationship will prosper, even if you are not the one who is changing.

If we want our marriage to remain vital, interesting, and fun, we need to keep the openness and adventuresome qualities of the young at heart. Oftentimes, over the years, we become rigid and stuck in our ways. Then when one partner attempts to grow or to try something new or different, conflict arises, forcing the other partner to decide whether to go on with the original agreement of the marriage or to work on coming up with a new one.

Such situations can be great opportunities to open up new lines of communion and communication, especially in long marriages or partnerships. If the agreements that you made about the relationship years ago no longer apply because of changes and growth along the way, then you both need to sit down and rewrite them. All life is change, say the Taoists. We cannot avoid change. We can only find our way to flow with it or else fight a losing battle trying to avoid or stop it.

Constancy, Flexibility, Open-Mindedness

Learning to be in relationship is often like learning a musical instrument. It takes time, patience, and the willingness to make unpleasant sounds in the beginning. Lao Tzu says:

> To know harmony is to know constancy.
> Knowing constancy is to be enlightened.
> *(Chapter 55)*

The following poem of mine addresses just this dynamic of constancy in relationship:

> Constancy requires a firm hand on the heart,
> an ongoing view of the big picture,
> a willingness to live in the present moment,
> a gentle letting go of needs and wants,
> the ability to love deeply and well,
> a strong sense of self,
> a true sense of being grounded and rooted
> in our body and being,
> an appreciation of small things,
> a feeling of lightness and ease within oneself,
> a strong feeling of devotion and
> connection to the divine—

both within ourselves and within our lover,
the ability to trust and be trusted,
an openness to change in every moment,
the understanding that not doing
is as important as doing,
an openness to both pain and joy,
a strong desire to surrender—
to our lover, to our life,
to the divine nature of the universe,
the releasing of all expectations,
and lastly,
a true sense of
what is important and what is not,
and then, to be able to
disregard what is not
and cherish what is.

In today's fast-paced world many people have a difficult time finding the time to cultivate themselves, never mind cultivating a relationship. The secret, though, is not the quantity of cultivation, but the quality. Constancy is the key to cultivating a healthy relationship and a long-lasting marriage.

Being consistently flexible, tolerant, emotionally and intellectually open, and willing to respect each other's cycles, both emotional and physical, are also keys to a successful marriage.

Remaining flexible and open-minded ensures that we are always open to new ideas and new experiences, which love and relationship are certainly always bringing us. Any long-term marriage or relationship gives us the opportunity to grow, both emotionally and spiritually. It offers myriad lessons, countless challenges, and numerous occasions to reflect on our own desires, dreams, and visions. Again, by treating your marriage as an opportunity for self-cultivation, you can benefit both yourself and your partner. By looking at your marriage as an opportunity for mutual growth, you will both grow together.

It is also very important to accept the other person in their entirety—with all their most wonderful attributes as well as their irritating faults. It is not necessary to point out these faults, but it is important to look deeply inside yourself to really see if you can be okay with them. If they seem too much or too deep or too strong, perhaps this is not the right person for you. It is equally important to acknowledge your own faults.

Merely staying in a marriage is not good enough to sustain a sacred union or spiritual marriage. Often people stay together for years in an unhappy and unhealthy marriage out of fear of being alone. But being alone and whole is never as damaging as being together in constant conflict or outright abuse.

In the long run, marriage or any long-term relationship gives us the opportunity to grow, both emotionally and spiritually. It offers myriad lessons, countless challenges, and numerous occasions to reflect on our own desires, dreams, and visions. Being successful in marriage is much like being successful in life. As the Beatles said, "The love you take is equal to the love you make!"

11

the tai chi of communion

Tai Ji calms and collects. It clears and sharpens the mind to help us in focusing and centering our daily activities. When the body and mind move harmoniously together, the human spirit soars.

CHUNGLIANG AL HUANG, *TAI JI*

MANY PEOPLE IN the West are familiar with the slow-moving, dancelike set of movements called tai chi chuan *(taiji quan)*. Not as many people realize that it is a form of chi gong. Like other forms of chi gong, it works with the principles of rootedness, balance, and a smooth flow of energy throughout the body. It is at once a playful dance of yin/yang and a powerful form of self-defense. It is a way to find your own moving center and to harmonize your being.

I suffered from chronic fatigue syndrome for over ten years. This is a seriously debilitating disease which Western medicine has no treatment for, never mind a cure. It is not only a matter of being tired. It is a bone-heavy sense of utter weakness and helplessness. Along with the fatigue come many other symptoms, such as blurred vision, insomnia, depression, fibromyalgia, unclear thinking, and short-term memory loss, among others. The doctors I saw at the time did lots of blood tests on me, and then when they could not find anything this way, they pronounced me healthy. When I told them that I was obviously very sick, they intimated that it was all in my head and perhaps I should be seeing a counselor instead of doctors.

After searching for help for years, I discovered Chinese medicine. Chinese herbs and then chi gong practice is what allowed me to have a life again. Now, a person who used to plan for weeks in advance to go to Portland, two hours away, leads tours to the sacred mountains of China as well as to the roof of the world, Tibet.

But perhaps the most important thing that this journey took me to was the discovery of Taoism. When I decided to look into the philosophical background of the type of medicine I was using, I found Taoism. It was like coming home. Now I write books such as the one you are reading, and have been publishing *The Empty Vessel*, a Taoist journal, since 1993.

The study of the Way gave me a ground upon which to build a solid spiritual and philosophical foundation. Its insights, teachings, and practices gave me tools to do the work it took to drag myself out of my deep depression and fear and to begin to live in the world of light again. Its practices such as tai chi, meditation, and chi gong gave me strength to come into my body in a much stronger and more grounded and even graceful way than I had ever experienced before.

The teachings and practices of Taoism have informed every aspect of my life, including my love life. It is in gratitude to what I have learned and the great influence that these teaching practices have had in my world of relationship that I have written this book so you too may benefit and prosper from these wise and wonderful teachings.

Studying Tai Chi

It has become relatively easy to find a tai chi instructor in any town of moderate size in the West; many community colleges and community centers employ them. The challenge is finding a good one. Make it a point to visit at least one class before deciding to make a commitment to a teacher. Be sure that the teacher is clear in his or her directions and that he or she offers good, nonjudgmental support for the students.

You may choose to study with a traditional Chinese teacher, as I did in my early days of tai chi. The traditional style of teaching offers little in the way of detailed instruction. Instead the student is told to follow the teacher's movement as best they can, with the idea that, with time, they will learn to embody the movements themselves. I would not recommend this style of learning for most people, but often, by following a true master, one can pick up an amazing amount of information with no verbal interaction at all.

Tai chi is not just about moving your body in elegant circles. It is about being able to tap into the very flow of the universe, the dance of energy as it moves through your being and as it is expressed by you personally. Each movement is designed to move the energy in your meridians and through your body, in a unique and very precise way. In the beginning, it is very important to understand the basic principles of tai chi and to be able to build upon them so that your practice becomes a manifestation of your own personal energy system. To force yourself to move in a way that is unnatural for you is a waste of time and can even be dangerous. Find a teacher who can pass on the principles and the postures in such a way that you can make them your own, through practice, through perseverance, through a discovery of your own nature. Then you can find your own expression of tai chi, of Tao itself.

In tai chi practice we learn how to push forward and how to yield; how to balance, first on one foot then the other; how to sink our energy deep within our bellies, our dan tian; how to maintain our composure, our inner stillness, even while moving. This is why tai chi is often called "stillness within movement." It is a wonderful way to learn how to maintain our still place within the oftentimes-challenging vicissitudes of life.

You can make your tai chi practice an integral part of your life by applying the lessons you learn there to your daily experience. Tai chi can help us learn to respond to life in a balanced and harmonious way, using the yin/yang energies in a flowing and spontaneous manner. We can apply the lessons we learn in tai chi practice to our love life. Let's look at some of the basic principles of tai chi and see how they relate to life and the art of relationship.

Centeredness

By learning through tai chi how to keep a calm and balanced center while moving backward and forward, from side to side, and sometimes in a complete circle, we can learn how to maintain a sense of centeredness in the rest of our lives.

When we have a strong sense of our center, even if things are moving all around us, we will be much more successful in many aspects of our life, including our love life. When we are off center, when we rely on our partner for our center, or when we rely on our job, our business, or our health condition for our center, we leave ourselves open to being knocked off center very easily. This can happen many times a day, not only when we are having an actual fight or argument with our partner. It can happen with a look that we feel is hostile or a few words we may take the wrong way or some small criticism we may feel as an all-out assault. It is very easy to become hurt or frightened or even angry when we are constantly being knocked off our center.

When we are connected to our center, we feel solid and rooted to the earth and to our own spiritual self. When we are centered, the winds may blow, the rain may fall, the lightening may flash, the thunder may crash, but we will still feel strong and whole. It is a little like being one of those funny toys we had in the fifties—a big plastic clown, which was weighted in the bottom. The game was to knock it over only to see it pop back up again. Being centered is a bit like being that plastic clown. When life's challenges come along to knock us over, we are able to pop right back up again instead of lying on the ground and whining.

The trick is to make sure that our sense of centeredness is not reliant upon someone or something else *outside* of us. It needs to come from deep within—that place where we are connected to our own sense of the divine, by whatever name you call it. For when people have no connection to the eternal in their being, then they can be knocked off center very easily. If they spend their time just doing their job and then spend the evening watching television and ignoring their partner and then either crash into their bed to snore the night away or perhaps have five or ten minutes of masturbatory sex with each other, then they will certainly reach the dark night of the soul when their job or their health or even their partner is taken away from them. They will feel lost and abandoned and desperately afraid.

Balance

Some of the movements in the tai chi form require that we lift one leg and balance on the other. Sometimes we are even required to kick out with one leg without losing our balance. We move up and down, back and forth, in different directions, all the while maintaining our sense of balance, poise, and rootedness.

Being in balance means being in harmony within our own being (see chapter 2). We cannot really attain harmony with another person unless we have some measure of it within ourselves. If we rely too much on others for our sense of harmony, we will often be disappointed.

In tai chi we practice balancing our weight on one foot at a time so the other foot is free to move in a new direction. In our emotional life it is also very helpful to have at least one emotional foot securely balanced on the ground. This way we will be able to move another part of ourselves into new or challenging territory without losing our sense of balance.

Being in harmony with our partner is a wonderful, pleasurable thing. It can make many of the challenges of life seem much easier to handle. It can keep us healthy. It can allow each of us in the partnership to open and flower in our own way. But it is very difficult to come into and remain in this state of harmony without a sense of balance in our emotions and energetic patterns. Remember, to Taoists, emotions are considered energetic states. I think most of us have experienced our emotions coming up suddenly, like a sudden storm. We have experienced the fierce winds and gales that emotions can create in us. We are knocked off balance and into a state of fear or anger or judgment in an instant. If we are able to find our balance again, hopefully before we have done too much damage to our partner or ourselves, then we can find ourselves sailing in calm waters again, under a bright sun in the blue sky.

How do we refind our balance? One way is to have some sense of objectivity. When we are caught up in our emotions of fear or anger, we lose all objectivity, and we see the problem or the other person as an insurmountable cliff. We are so sure of ourselves in our delusion. It is only later, after we have calmed down, that we begin to see that our emotions clouded our heart or mind, and we were lost at sea. If we can cultivate a sense of objectivity, we will be able find our way back to the calm waters much more quickly.

In order to cultivate objectivity, we need to employ what we can call the "watcher" or the "observer." This observer is the one who can take a step back from the center of the storm and watch it with a dispassionate eye. Most of us know what this feels like, as most of us have done it, though usually after the fact. The observer or watcher is the one who can laugh at our fears and foibles. It is the one who takes the long view instead of the short. It is the one who, in the midst of the emotional roller coaster, can remind us that we have been through similar storms before and lived through them. Or it can show us that, compared with what else is going on in our lives, this present moment is but one moment. Or it can remind us that, contrary to what we are feeling, we have the opportunity to learn about ourselves in a new way.

The observer is the part of our self that can just watch what is going on and say, "Oh, here I am doing this again." Or, "Here I am being carried away with myself again." Or, "It sure is interesting how I fall into this pattern over and over again. I wonder what it would be like to *not* fall into it but try something new."

It is in being able to have some objectivity that we are able to take that crucial step backward and out of the immediate situation and remind ourselves that we will *not* actually die from it but, just like the last dozen times we did this, actually go on to live another day.

Objectivity is crucial if we are to live our lives in some balance and harmony. I once read a book on new physics that talked about how, when we watch a film at a theater or on a television set, we get so swept up into the story that we see only the events on the screen as they play themselves out there. We no longer see the screen or the area outside of the screen. But if we take a step back and refocus our eyes to see what is outside the screen, we are no longer so involved emotionally with what is happening on it.

The same is true in our lives. If, when we are all caught up in an emotional situation, we take a step back, emotionally and energetically, we will suddenly see the big picture and not be so swept away by the moment. We will then be able to find a new perspective of the situation and perhaps a different response. Then the balance that we need to live a more harmonious life with our partner and, more importantly, with ourselves, will naturally arise.

Receiving with Emptiness

When using tai chi for self-defense, we use the principle of emptiness: when someone strikes a blow at us, we can sink or turn at just the right moment so the blow is met by empty space. A true tai chi master will not allow him- or herself to be struck by an opponent. By subtly twisting and moving out of the way, they do not provide any surface for the blows of the opponent to connect.

In a relationship, we can apply the principle of emptiness when we feel criticized or verbally abused by our partner. If we hold ourselves in our center and are able to meet an attack with emptiness, then it cannot hurt us. Instead of letting the words into our emotional body, where they can cause us much pain, we are able to neutralize them. Then we can examine our partner's words dispassionately, looking at where they are valid and where we may feel they are not. If we do not immediately assume a defensive posture or go on the attack ourselves, a heated moment can be defused much easily.

At first, not verbally defending ourselves or firing back harsh words will be very challenging, and we will not always succeed. But with perseverance, it will become second nature.

An argument in which both sides are feeling aggressive and defensive can often escalate until one or both say or do things they later regret. By using the tai chi principles of deflecting negative energy with emptiness, the confrontation can often be defused much more easily.

What this means is when someone comes at you with anger or negative energy, instead of investing in the negative energy yourself, you simply relax and let their negativity flow over you like water. As you relax, you must also regard your partner with compassion. They may have a good reason, at least in their mind, to attack you this way. You can hear them out, see where your own fault lies, and then respond to them, not with more negativity but with compassion and understanding. In this way, you do not get caught up in the negativity yourself but are able to maintain your own center.

It is important to not be drawn into our partner's negative state. If you can keep your equilibrium and not get caught up in the drama, while being compassionate and emotionally supportive, you can often allow your partner to work through their negativity or fear more quickly. It will also be helpful if you don't attempt to be too helpful. Being supportive is one thing, but trying to fix the situation or emotion, unless asked to do so by your partner, will only make things worse. Allowing your partner the time and space to work through their negative state in a way that works for them will usually end up being the best thing. If they do ask for your help or input, by all means give it, without judgment or blame, if at all possible.

My teacher, Hua-Ching Ni, talks about being "an emotional simpleton." This means that when someone tries to hurt your feelings, complains about you, or verbally attacks you, you react very slowly, not instantly rising to a defense or attack. Instead you allow time to go by; you formulate your thoughts about the matter very slowly and deliberately. You forgive others quickly and readily.

Becoming an emotional simpleton allows you to be immune to the negative energy of others. You live in your own world, where everything is positive and everyone is your friend. Not that you let people walk all over you; instead, as an emotional simpleton, you do not even *notice* when you are being attacked. Instead, you have faith that all emotional turmoil will balance itself, either on its own or by you not adding more fuel to the fire.

As Master Ni says in *Moonlight in the Dark Night:*

> An emotional simpleton is not sensitive to unimportant
> things. An emotional simpleton does not know how to
> complain about unimportant details and does not remember
> what minor trouble people have caused. By learning this
> small skill of being an emotional simpleton and applying it
> in the correct instance, you will have the entire world for our
> spiritual joy, privacy, and cultivation. *(Chapter 2)*

Gracefulness

Gracefulness is one of the most powerful effects of tai chi practice. Being a bit of a late bloomer, I didn't start practicing tai chi until I was in my thirties, but when I did, I felt, for the first time in my life, a sense of grace in my movements. I had never been a dancer and had spent much of my life in my head, and tai chi was a wonderful tool to get me down into my body in a gentle and graceful way.

If someone spends too much time in their head and too little time in their energy/emotional body, it is very easy for them to get off balance and to feel easily threatened. Then if they do not have a sense of grace in themselves and their life, they will react to others with anger and hostility, mostly due to fear. At the same time, they will feel awkward and unsure of themselves emotionally and so will lash out at their partner. It is very easy, when feeling awkward and tight, to simply transfer the weight onto the other person and blame them.

But if one *does* have a sense of grace in their lives, as well as in their emotional body, they will better be able to shift with the cycles of change, both internally and externally. With grace comes a feeling of self-worth and self-esteem. These are valuable things indeed. With a strong sense of self-esteem, one can weather all kinds of emotional storms and challenges and not be engulfed by them.

Rootedness

Rootedness is important in the flowing movements of tai chi. We always move from a sense of rootedness, both to the earth under our feet and within our own body. This need for rootedness applies equally to our emotional life as well. When we are rooted and stable in our own heart center, it is not so easy to knock us off base. And if we can combine rootedness with centeredness, with the weighted bottom of the clown toy mentioned earlier, we can bounce right back when we get knocked over by the challenges of life.

One of the things that struck me first about Taoist practices when I discovered them was how grounded they are in the earth. They are not about getting up and out of the body, but rather, for the most part, are concerned with becoming as rooted and grounded as possible.

Taoism honors the earth, and many of the practices are about going down and into the watery, mysterious, yin nature of both the earth and our own being. It is in our sense of rootedness or groundedness that we can connect with our essential nature, that part of us that is the most real, that part of ourselves that is the most high and precious, that part of ourselves that is always safe and secure and does not easily dissolve into fear or anger.

When we think of what a tree looks like, what we usually envision is only the top part of the tree, the part that we can see *above* the ground.

In actuality, there is a whole other part of the tree that lives *under*-ground. With its many roots and rootlets all fanning out underneath it, sometimes over quite a large area, the tree has a mirror image below ground. When we are able to look at a tree and envision what it really looks like, with both its yin or earth side and its yang or sky side, then we can say we are able to really see a tree.

So too do we humans live our lives, partway externally, out in the world, and partway internally, with our feelings, thoughts, and energetic tides. If we can feel ourselves rooted in the earth like a tree, perhaps we can then experience ourselves and others as much more multidimensional beings.

In Taoism, it is not enough to just *imagine* ourselves rooted; we need to actually *experience* it. The way we do this is to really dig down energetically into the earth and allow ourselves to really feel it. We can either sit or stand and just experience ourselves in this way, or we can practice drawing up sustenance and healing from the earth, just like a tree or other plant does. It is only when we truly feel this rootedness in the earth in our own body that we will understand what it means.

Then whenever we feel as though we are about to topple over or be blown away in an emotional gale, we can stop and send these roots down again so we can once again feel ourselves as solid, grounded, and rooted beings.

↻ Rooting Exercise

Here is a simple exercise in grounding that you may find helpful.

Sit or stand with your legs shoulder-width apart. If you are sitting on a chair, sit on the edge of the chair. If you are sitting on the floor, be sure and put a cushion under your spine so you will be supported there. Close your eyes and breathe, slowly and deeply, through your nose.

Spend a few moments doing this, relaxing your whole body from the top of your head to the bottoms of your feet.

Then energetically send down roots, as if you were a tree, down from the bottom of your feet if you are standing or sitting on the edge of a chair or from the base of your spine if you are sitting on a cushion. Send them down deep, at least five lengths of your body. Feel them burrowing down through the earth, down past all the other tree roots, stones, animal burrows, and so on. Once you can feel them reach all the way down into the earth, stop and just feel yourself there, rooted solidly like a tree. Feel how the wind may blow the top part of you around, but the rest of you remains firmly rooted in the earth. Feel yourself sending your limbs out into the sky while at the same time feel your roots burrowing deeper and deeper into the earth.

Once you have gotten them as far as you can, sit or stand with that image, that feeling, pulling energy from deep within the earth up through your tailbone or the bottoms of your feet. See your roots as strong and healthy. Feel yourself as a tree, reaching out toward the sun while remaining solidly rooted in the earth.

When you are ready, pull those roots back up toward your body, while retaining the feeling of being a deeply rooted tree.

You can use this rooting image with your partner as well, sending your roots together into the earth and mingling your roots with each other's to support the great tree of your relationship.

Naturalness

Naturalness is another important Taoist principle in tai chi practice, as well as in daily life. The more natural we are, the more we will be in touch with our own authentic or spiritual nature.

What does this mean, to maintain the natural wholeness of our spirits? One thing it can be referring to is how well we are able to unite our various energetic, emotional, and psychological bodies into one unified whole. Taoists believe that we as individuals are really a grouping of souls or spirits, called the *hun* and the *po*. Just as we have different moods and thoughts and ideas throughout one day, so too are we comprised of many different spiritual energies. It is in cultivating our ability to unify these various energies, moods, and emotions into a unified field that we can truly experience what it is like to live as what the Chinese call zhen ren (tzu ran), or an authentic or realized being. This state may also be thought of as what the Buddhists and other Eastern religions call enlightenment.

In the world of relationship, the Taoist understanding of naturalness says that to try to bend yourself out of shape, to bend contrary to your own nature, to appease or to be accepted by someone else will end in disaster. Either your own true nature will assert itself eventually or you will end up bent into so many unnatural angles that you will become an emotional pretzel. When this happens, you end up shutting down your own natural being and will become stunted emotionally as well as energetically.

The question is, can the other person in the relationship accept you as you are, in your own natural being, or must you try to become someone else to please or win them? While you want to be on your best behavior, especially in a new relationship, eventually you must decide if you can still be in a particular relationship when you are being yourself.

Instead of trying too hard to talk someone else into what you want, try to become someone whose wishes are infectious. Instead of trying to get someone else to change their thinking, be so sure and so enthusiastic about your way of seeing that they will naturally be more open to seeing things as you do. This is the wu wei style of communication indeed!

Flexibility

Flexibility, as mentioned in chapter 10, is an important concept in Taoism, as well as in tai chi. The supple bamboo that bends with the wind survives the storm much more easily than the stiff oak. It is when we are too tightly wound and unable to flow with a situation that we end up in trouble. Being in relationship requires endless adjustments, some small, some large. It is in our ability and willingness to enter that flow with another that we can be successful and happy in relationship.

Say you have an evening planned with your partner. You have been looking forward to it all day, and when the time comes, you are all primed and ready to go. But suddenly your partner's mood has changed, or they are not feeling well, or something at work or in their own personal life has come up, and they are not able to go with the earlier plan. You could choose to get upset or bent out of shape (that pretzel again). You may end up having an argument or even a fight with them, which only makes you both feel even worse.

How different would it be to be able to flow with the currents of the situation and be flexible enough to let the other person off the hook with no blame, no shame? You may still be disappointed that the evening plan has been changed, but because of your ability to flow and be flexible, you find something else to do with your partner or, if they need to go off and do something else, to do alone, with pleasure.

Being flexible and going with the change in flow is very different from stuffing our feelings and creating a world of resentment toward our partner. It means truly being able to change our flow to harmonize with the greater flow. If we can learn to do this in small ways, then perhaps we can move onto bigger things. One thing for sure, life will always give us many opportunities for this kind of cultivation.

As mentioned earlier, Taoist teachings concern themselves very much with cycles of change and transformation. In these cycles, we see that our own energy—be that emotional, psychological, or physical—changes and shifts throughout the day and evening. Multiply those shifts by days and weeks and years, and we can get a sense that much of our life is constantly shifting and moving and transforming. The more aware we can be of these shifts, the more flexible we can be, the more open to flowing with the moment we can be, the happier and healthier we will be.

Physically too, we need to maintain our flexibility. A stiff, armored body does not lend itself well to juicy, extended Taoist lovemaking. Practices such as yoga, *Tao in* (a type of Taoist yoga), chi gong, and tai chi are wonderful ways to keep our bodies young and flexible. As mentioned in chapter 10, we must also keep ourselves flexible in our thoughts and emotions. A true mark of growing old is when we start to shut down internally as well as externally. Without a strong sense of flexibility, we cannot maintain a healthy relationship.

Yielding

There are many moves in tai chi where we move forward—sometimes with a punch or a kick and sometimes just a gentle push. At other times, we yield and pull our energy back. Yielding can be used in a combat situation; by allowing our opponent to rush ahead, we can, with a gentle application, use their own momentum to deflect their blows or even throw them across the room.

It is when we attempt to meet force with force, as when we have a disagreement or argument with our partner, that we end up wasting a lot of time and energy. Fighting fire with fire only makes a bigger fire. This is not to say that you don't have a right to stick up for yourself. If you truly disagree with your partner, it is fine to voice that disagreement. But if you are attached to changing the other person's mind or convincing them that you are right and they are wrong, you will get nowhere.

Conflict is inevitable. Anyone who doesn't realize that will never last in a long-term relationship. It is in how we respond and react to conflict that will decide if the union will last or not. Reacting in an extreme way to any kind of conflict only fuels the fire of disharmony.

Problems can be handled or often even solved by a variety of methods. There is no one method or technique that works for every conflict every time. By taking the time to examine the energetic aspects of each situation, we can then take the appropriate yin or yang approach. Forcing is always followed by loss of strength. This is not the way of Tao.

Trying to outshout or outsmart our partner will never work. By applying the yin/yang principle of tai chi, we can become better at steering toward a harmonious outcome when conflict does arise. Do not meet a yang force with a yang force. It will only make matters worse. To put out a fire, use water, not more fire! Instead, try deflecting the attack with a soft, yin approach. Instead of fueling the argument, try backing off. Instead of trying to make the other person wrong, admit your own mistakes right away. This doesn't mean caving in to another's unrealistic demands; it means that you are taking the time to see the other person's side of things.

Lao Tzu says:

> The softest thing under heaven
> Overcomes the hardest thing under heaven.
> *(Chapter 43)*

Chuang Tzu, the most influential Taoist master after Lao Tzu, says:

> Suppose that you and I argue. If you win and I lose, does
> that mean that you are right and I am wrong? And if I win
> and you lose, does that mean that I am right and you are
> wrong? Or are we both partly right and partly wrong? Or can
> we both be right as well as wrong? In other words, does win-
> ning an argument mean that one is right? And does losing
> one mean that one is wrong? Is it not true that some people
> are just better at arguing? To try to control someone else
> physically or even emotionally goes against the Tao and will
> end in suffering for both parties. *(Chapter 2)*

It is in giving up the need to be right that we are freed from turmoil in our relationship. It is in giving up being the one who is control that we liberate ourselves. It is in giving up the idea of always knowing what is right from what is wrong that we release ourselves from our overburdened, intellectual mind.

If we are the type of person who looks at the world for differences, we will always see those differences. But if we become a person who sees the world for sameness, then everything we see will be in harmony and agreement with our own inner being.

transitions

beginnings and endings

*If an unbalanced person is leaning on something, and that something
goes away, the unbalanced person will fall. It is that kind of reliance
or expectation towards someone else that causes the broken heart.*

HUA-CHING NI, *MOONLIGHT IN THE DARK NIGHT*

Beginning a Relationship

There is nothing that can compare with new love for putting a sparkle
in your eye and a bounce in your step. It can be one of the most exciting and life-changing experiences possible. When you are newly in love,
the whole world seems a much brighter and better place. You walk
around with a smile on your face and a warm feeling in your heart.

But even at the best of times, new love can take a lot of work to
cultivate. Here we can use the image of a garden. In order to grow
things, we must till the ground, open it, and make it ready to receive
the seeds that will produce the sweet food that we may eat and enjoy.
Then, after the seeds have been planted, we must take gentle and
tender care of our plants, watering them fully with our tears of joy

and sorrow. We must also fertilize the soil in order for the plants to grow straight and strong.

Then we must be patient. It takes time to grow a good crop, and trying to hurry anything will not help. There is an old Chinese folktale about the farmer, who, after noticing that his neighbor's garden was growing much faster than his, went out in the night and tugged on all his plants so that they would grow faster. When he went out the next morning, they were all lying lifeless on the ground.

So too can it take time to grow a relationship. And, as with the garden, it takes much tender and patient energy before a relationship can truly bear fruit and produce the luscious crop that we want to enjoy. If our intent is really to achieve the Tao of intimacy and ecstasy, then we must be able to be patient, both with the other person and with ourselves. By letting things grow in a gradual fashion, we will be able to create a strong foundation to build a sacred union on. By rushing into something too fast, the foundation will not be there for when the more difficult times come, as they almost always do.

It also helps not to have too much of an agenda. By this I mean not to be too pushy with what we want to be happening or wish were happening. If we cannot accept and be turned on to the person right in front of us right now, then how can we hope to build a lasting or deep relationship with them in the future? This is especially important for men to remember. As mentioned earlier, man is the quickly flaring fire, and woman is the slowly bubbling water. If a man is too pushy with a woman at the beginning, either by pressing for sex before the woman is ready or by trying to force the relationship to flower too quickly, then the relationship is doomed to fail.

Taoism teaches us that using force to try to attain the outcome we desire will only backfire. Here the principle of wu wei, or "not doing anything against the natural order," comes into play. It can also mean not doing anything against your own nature. And even when discovering our true nature, we must go slowly and with exquisite sensitivity. Just as in the Taoist sexual practices, we need to be able to move slowly so that both sides, both individuals' true natures, can come to their own fruition in the most natural and beneficial way.

Trying to hurry or force a relationship kills its spirit, and a relationship will either fail or never fully develop. If we move slowly and with the right amount of sensitivity and openness, it can have the time to grow into a beautiful flower.

Sometimes it happens that two people meet each other, and because of some past-life connection or karmic destiny or just plain great energy together, it works out for them to move rather quickly. But even in this situation, it is extremely important to take time to do the deep work that it takes to reach the Tao of intimacy and ecstasy. In these cases, it is very important to be very upfront with our feelings, our fears, our desires, our dreams and wishes and to share these things right away. In this way, even though the building is going fast, we can erect, brick by brick, the beautiful shining tower of our love and deep devotion, our sacred union.

Another extremely important thing at the beginning of a relationship is to practice being present at all times and in all situations. By this I mean to be totally present or at least to the best of our abilities, in any moment. If we are living in the past or daydreaming of the future all the time, then we do not pay close enough attention to what is happening right in front of us. Whether the moment is a beautiful one or a difficult one, it is only in being as present and fully focused as possible that we can experience it in all of its power and grace.

It is said that the present is the point of power. All of our decisions that will affect our future are made in the present moment. It is the decisions and the actions that we take now that will create the future we want or do not want. This does not mean that we cannot plan for the future or keep our fond memories of the past. But if they drag us away from the present too often and too strongly, then we will be wasting this precious time of the present.

By being strongly and solidly in the moment, we can better truly hear what the other person is saying or trying to communicate in some other way. We can be less judgmental, less fearful perhaps, and less demanding. It is almost impossible to really hear someone else while our mind or energy is elsewhere.

Yesterday has already gone and tomorrow has not yet arrived. All we have is a series of ever-shifting todays, each present moment filled with possibility and grace. By living in the present moment as much as possible, we can let go of worry about the future, of endless regrets about the past. We can sink deep roots of being and of opening to the other as we begin to discover who the other person is, who we are with them, and who we are together.

In addition to being present, being aware and sensitive to the balance and subtle shifts of our own yin and yang qualities, as well as internal energetic/emotional ebbs and flows, will allow us to make proper decisions and conduct ourselves with greater integrity and foresight in our dealings with others.

It is also very important to be accepting of the other person, with all their most wonderful attributes as well as their irritating faults. It is not necessary to point out these faults or try to correct them, but it is necessary to look deeply inside yourself to really see if you can be okay with them. If they seem too much or too deep or too strong, perhaps this is not the right person for you. It is also important that you are able to acknowledge your own faults. Remember, harmony is a critical aspect of the Tao of intimacy and ecstasy. If there is no harmony or if you fall out of harmony with each other, it can harm the relationship, even fatally. (More on this later in the chapter.)

The key to happiness in a relationship is flexibility and open-mindedness. If we cultivate these qualities in ourselves, we are always open to the new ideas and new experiences our partner can offer. At the same time, we need to have a deep appreciation of what we can offer. If we want something to last, we must give deeply of ourselves. We must dig down into the very deepest part of our soul and offer forth the shining pearl that we are!

By remembering and using the principles of being present, of wu wei or not forcing, of not having too strong an agenda, and of being able to accept the person for who they are right now, rather than who we might hope they will become in some illusory future, we can build a strong foundation for a beautiful and strong union.

All of this can be very difficult for young people, whose energies and hormones are raging. It can be much easier for a middle-aged or otherwise mature person. Nevertheless, it is important that anyone really interested in the Tao of intimacy and ecstasy, at whatever age they may be, look at these principles.

Ending a Relationship

One of the statistics that gets bandied about these days is much higher divorce rates than in the 1930s and 1940s. This increase is often attributed to the more open and free-wheeling attitude of baby boomers (those of us in our fifties and sixties). It is most often seen as a negative thing, but I am not convinced it is.

Perhaps modern people have a much more developed sense of self-worth and of what a good relationship can be like. The old adage "We must stay together for the children" is no longer so accepted. Even if it is extremely challenging for children when their parents break up, it can be even more painful for them to live in a household with parents who fight all the time, are cold and distant from each other, or are just not very loving to one another.

Ending a relationship is often a very painful, heartrending experience. It can call up the very worst in a person and turn what was once a beautiful friendship into a source of pain and anger. And while hurt, angry, and sad feelings are usually unavoidable, there are a few ways that we can still end a relationship in a conscious manner.

The first important thing is to come to a decision about whether it is time to end the relationship. If you are spending more time fighting than loving each other; if you have such radically different approaches to life that there is no meeting place between you; if there is abuse of any kind, be it physical, emotional, or psychological; if there is unfaithfulness, lying, or an unwillingness to work on core issues, then the best thing would be to end the relationship. If either one or both of your personalities or outlooks on life change so radically that the relationship is no longer harmonious and perhaps even becomes unhealthy, then it is time to end the relationship and let each other go, in light and love, and move on with your lives.

Not every relationship is meant to last a lifetime. Oftentimes two people are meant to be together to clear up some sort of karmic debt or to give birth to and raise children together. Then, when the children are raised or the karmic debt has been paid off, they are free to move on to another part of their lives.

Often, at the end of a relationship, especially if it is a challenging break, we will feel perfectly justified to hold a lot of anger and hate. Unfortunately, this will only impede our own healing and make it more difficult to move on with our lives.

Our identity is often so intertwined with our partner that once that bond is broken, we really don't have a clear sense of who we are any more. Spending time alone, time exploring, and time in deep meditation and reflection can be so helpful in this case. Learning to know and love ourselves again will go a long way to helping us create a new relationship when we are ready.

The principle of the Watercourse Way can also be helpful at such times. The ability to go with the flow and the all-important ability to be flexible and adapt to any situation will help us so much. Taoists call spiritual work "self-cultivation." We continually plant small seeds of spiritual growth in the soil of our experience. Then, with much patience and care, those small seeds will sprout into beautiful flowerings. Every situation in our lives, both good and bad, is a part of that cultivation. Even the most negative experiences, including the ending of a relationship, can be used as mulch or compost in cultivating the garden of our self.

13

energy is delight

the world of chi gong

Chi gong is a series of movements, both internal and external, that directly activates or helps a smooth flow of chi or vital force throughout the body.

HUA-CHING NI, *THE GENTLE PATH OF SPIRITUAL PROGRESS*

THE TERM *CHI gong* is made of two Chinese characters. The first one, *chi,* is the basic life force of the universe; it is what animates us, what warms us, keeps our organs in their places, and directs all of our movements. The character *gong* means "work," or something that takes effort and time. Thus, the term *chi gong* means working with your energy, work that will take a lot of effort and time to become fruitful.

While some types of chi gong do not include outward movement, most of them consist of some kind of movement, both internal and external, in order to strengthen and harmonize one's internal energy. There are many different types of chi gong, some quite vigorous and some sublimely simple. All chi gong styles deal with accessing, circulating, and storing chi or vital force, within the body. The effects of doing chi gong will vary from person to person, according to the skill level of the practitioner, the consistency of the practice, and the practitioner's age and relative health.

It is beyond the scope of this book to address the large and multilayered subject of chi gong thoroughly; however, more complete works on chi gong are now widely available. This chapter is a simple introduction to a vast and complex practice that has been in continuous practice in China for at least three thousand years and is still evolving today.

Chi gong is a way of creating harmony within ourselves. As mentioned earlier, if we are not in harmony with ourselves, then it is almost impossible to be in harmony with another, especially if that relationship is going to be one in which all our inner demons and worst habits will be found out.

Also, if we want to be able to practice the Tao of Sex, we need to be moderately healthy. If we are going to be able to be self-reliant and not drain our partner—emotionally, physically, or energetically—then we need to be both grounded and strong in our own being.

ῦ❧ Feeling Chi

An easy way to feel chi is to create a chi ball between your two palms. First rub your palms together until you feel some sense of heat. Then hold them out in front of you at shoulder or waist height. Imagine there is a solid ball of energy between them, about the size of a beach ball. Gently push your hands together, without allowing them to touch, squeezing the ball between them. Next, expand the ball by pulling your hands apart. Keep pushing your hands together and pulling them apart until it feels like there is some kind of pressure between them when you bring them together.

Do this simple exercise a few times and you will begin to feel a subtle yet solid, rubbery presence between your palms.

The Art of Chi Gong

As mentioned earlier, chi gong requires hard work and perseverance. Significant changes cannot be brought about in a single weekend workshop. It takes time to reroute the oftentimes unnatural flows of chi that have built up in our bodies. It can take years of practice to heal long-standing health problems or to build up enough vital chi so new health problems do not occur. It can take a lifetime of practice to be able to align one's chi with the chi of the universe and be able to transcend the physical world as we know it, at the point of death or before. But all along the way, there are rewards and benefits for anyone who pursues a regular practice.

The positive results can be of a physical, emotional, psychological, or spiritual nature or a combination of all four. Practicing chi gong will make you healthier, more emotionally centered, more psychologically balanced, more psychic, smarter, more attractive, more creative, and happier; it will strengthen your will and deepen your character. This may seem unbelievable, but it is indeed true. Long-term regular practice of any kind of chi gong can produce all of these results and more.

Extensive research is currently being conducted in China on the effects of chi gong practice. A study by the Physiological Research Group of Shanghai First Medical College shows that chi gong practice decreases blood pressure, decreases metabolic rate, and increases peristalsis. It also causes the sympathetic stress reaction to greatly relax. Chi gong is used regularly in hospitals all over China for the treatment of heart disease and cancer, as well as for many other illnesses.

All chi gong practice concerns accessing, circulating, and storing chi, as well as directing, tonifying, and building a strong current of chi in the body. The various chi pathways in the body range from major meridians, such as the du mo (flows up the back), the ren mo (flows down the front), the belt channel (flows around the waist), the chong mo (flows directly through the center of the body), the major yin channels (flow along the inside of the arms and legs), and the major yang channels (flow along the outside of the arms and legs).

Along those pathways are certain points that are used to either access or tonify the chi in that area. Several important points often used in chi gong practice are the bai hui point at the top of the head (the crown chakra), the *tian mu* point between the eyebrows (the third eye), the *shan zhong* point (the heart center), the *wei lu* point at the bottom of the sacrum, the *hui yin* point on the perineum, the *yong quan* points at the bottoms of the feet, and the *lao gong* points on the palms of the hands. When these points are energized and opened, the chi in the pathways can run more smoothly and stronger.

⚗ Center and Balance Chi

Here is another simple yet effective exercise. Stand quietly for a few moments, then bring your arms slowly up in front of you, palms facing down, to shoulder level. Slowly lower them to waist level. This movement raises your central chi to the heart center then back down to the lower dan tian. It is an effective way to balance and center your energy. Try doing the complete movement—arms from shoulder level to waist level and back again to shoulders—at least nine times and see if you feel a difference in your sense of balance and wellbeing.

There are also three major areas or dan tians in the body. *Dan* means "medicine," or "elixir," and *tien* means "field." The top dan tian is the third-eye area, including the pineal gland. The middle dan tian is the heart area around the solar plexus. The lower dan tian is three finger widths below the navel. All of these areas are located inside the body, rather than on the surface. As with the points, once these areas are stimulated and energized, the amount of chi available to the practitioner grows manyfold.

✤ Basic Chi Gong Breathing Practice

This is the basic chi gong breathing practice, and if done regularly, it will change how you breathe, even when you are asleep. Many of us spend a lot of time breathing in a shallow and stressful way, causing our nervous system to remain in a flight-or-fight mode. This breathing exercise can change that.

To begin, sit or lie down in a comfortable position. It is not necessary to sit in the full lotus or even half lotus, if these are too difficult. You can either sit cross-legged or on the edge of a chair. Just be sure to sit at the front edge of the chair with your feet flat on the floor. Keep your spine erect without being too stiff. Either close your eyes half way or all the way.

Begin breathing through your nose, slowly, deeply, and quietly. As you inhale, allow your abdomen to expand, and when you exhale, allow it to contract. Remember, it is always important to not try to force anything. This can cause energetic or even health problems. Just breathe slowly and deeply and allow your abdomen to move in and out, concentrating on your lower dan tian, in your lower abdomen.

Eventually you may begin to feel some sense of warmth or tingling in your lower abdomen. This is a good sign, because it means the chi is being activated there. Don't try to do anything with the sensation, but just let it naturally grow there. It will usually begin to move on its own to where it needs to go.

Chi gong also works with the chi field that is located both inside and outside the body. Passing your hands down the front or back of your body can affect your internal organs because of the relationship between the outer and inner chi field as we will see in the essence chi gong form in chapter 14. It also may explain how people described in the Bible were healed just by touching the hem of Jesus's robe. His energy field was apparently so strong that he didn't even have to be conscious of sending his healing chi out to affect someone.

Taoists see the human *(ren)* as the fulcrum between heavenly energy and earthly energy. This is why the arts of astrology and astronomy have played such an important role in Taoist science. A strong electromagnetic field produced by the planets and stars in the heavens exerts a powerful influence upon us humans, and the electromagnetic power of the earth itself also exerts a strong influence upon us. We receive heavenly energy through our bai hui point at the very top of the head; we receive earthly energy through our yong quan points at the bottoms of our feet, which are the beginnings of the kidney channel, also called the "bubbling well points." When we work to open and energize these points, we are better able to be a clear channel for heavenly and earthly energy, both for our own health and for healing others. That combined with the unimpeded circulation of chi in our bodies makes us strong, vital beings who can influence everyone around us.

Chi gong practice, which combines deep and regular breathing, slow movements, and visualization, can have a profound effect on our entire system. Breathing in a slow, deep fashion alone causes a shift in the autonomous nervous system from the chronically overactive sympathetic mode to a calm, restorative parasympathetic mode, thereby balancing and harmonizing the body's energies.

⚘ Connecting to the Chi of the Natural World

This exercise is done with a tree and is a way to connect to the chi of the natural world. As trees are of the wood element, this exercise is especially beneficial to your liver.

Stand with your back to a good-sized tree. Place your hands over your lower abdomen (your lower dan tian), fingers interlaced. Allow your breath to become very slow and deep, your abdomen expanding with each inhalation and contracting with each exhalation. Allow yourself to feel the tree "breathing" behind you.

Begin to imagine that you are exchanging chi with the tree. After a while of doing this, you should begin to feel a sense of energy moving between you and the tree. Continue the exchange for as long as feels comfortable.

As mentioned in chapter 6, it is said that "chi follows yi," meaning that chi can be directed by the mind. Ancient Taoists knew what modern Western science is only now discovering—that we can direct healing energy with our mind and affect the healing process. Experiments have been conducted in which practitioners send energy to a certain part of their bodies; that area is then measured with heat-sensitive instruments. Results have shown an increase in heat radiation in the area to which the practitioner has directed chi.

In the beginning stages of chi gong practice, we use our minds to gently guide or lead chi through the pathways and points we are working with. In the higher stages of practice, we cease even using the mind, simply letting the chi guide itself.

Chi gong practice not only aligns our own body, mind, and spirit, but also aligns us with the universal body-mind-spirit. By regulating our minds through meditation and gentle movement, we can facilitate a smoother and stronger flow of energy throughout our bodies, giving us greater health and freedom of movement throughout our lives.

Chi gong works with the forces of the universe in a clear-hearted and grounded manner in order to raise not only our own consciousness but also that of the planet itself.

Chi gong is a way to access the energy of the universe and make it our own. It is a way to open our spiritual eyes to be able to see beyond what our physical eyes can reach. It is an attentive, articulated attitude of openness and grace, an exchange of energy on a deep and basic level of our inner being with the great undivided, unending Tao. And with that exchange comes balance, harmony, composure of spirit, deepening of character, and a relaxing of the mind muscles. It brings a feeling of safety, of being at home, of being empty and full at the same time, of being attentive to detail and clear of vision, of being open-hearted, of being soft yet strong, like water, like wind. It brings sensitivity to changes in the energetic atmosphere, the simple joy in beingness, compassion for the suffering of those around you, a sense of proportion, objectivity, and an openness to change, transformation, and miracles.

Chi gong is actually an approach to life itself. It is state of mind characterized by complete relaxation and complete acceptance; deep meditation; love, joy, and beneficence; renewal and rebirth. It is open to the healing energy of the universe, and it offers healing for the whole world.

When we practice chi gong with the intention of not only healing ourselves but also becoming a healing influence on all those around us, we begin practicing high-level chi gong. One of my teachers likes to tell us that chi is love and that we practice chi gong so we can become healthier and stronger, which enables us to help others become stronger and healthier. Others are then freed to help others in an unbroken and endless chain of love and chi.

✤ Chi Gong Partner Exercise

Sit back-to-back with your partner. Let your hands
sit in your lap or palms up on your thighs. Begin to
breathe deeply and slowly with the basic chi gong
breath. As with the tree exercise, feel your partner's breath begin to harmonize with yours. Feel
their energy begin to flow into you as yours does
into them. Feel yourselves as one being, breathing
together as one.

This exercise is a good one to harmonize your
energies when one or both of you have been under a
lot of stress or if you feel that things are not in harmony between you.

Learning to Practice Chi Gong

There are currently many chi gong books and DVDs available, some of
very good quality. However, the best way to learn chi gong, like tai chi,
is from a live teacher, one who will guide you as you work with energy.
Having an in-person teacher is especially important for the beginning
levels. There is much that can be transmitted from person to person
that is all but impossible to get from a DVD or book.

It can be challenging to find a good chi gong teacher. When you are
interviewing a prospective teacher, it is important to ask about their
own experience. Find out how long they have been practicing chi gong,
if they practice daily, if they know something about the meridian system,
who their teacher was, and if they are properly certified to teach.

There are currently many false teachers both from China, as well as
from the West, who are claiming great powers of healing and promis-
ing, for a fee, to perform all sorts of miraculous treatments. When
someone seems to be charging an exorbitant rate and is making exorbitant claims, it could very well be that they are a fraud. Unfortunately,
most people in the West know very little, if anything, about chi gong

and chi gong healing techniques, and they can be taken advantage of very easily. Look to the appendix of this book for some organizations that can help you find a teacher or healer in your area.

It is challenging for most people to muster the will needed to keep up a daily practice for years. Nowadays it is all too simple to become involved with various religious or New Age practices in a shallow and casual way. One day you're a Buddhist, the next a Sufi, the next you're channeling space beings. By contrast, chi gong cultivation is a long and often slow path with inevitable bends and twists. It takes total commitment and lots of hard work to reach the highest levels of attainment. Most people are happy just to get some relief from their health issues, clear up their psychological or emotional issues, and perhaps gain some spiritual insight into their lives. This is all fine. However, if you are truly serious about transcending the ties of the material world and "flying on the back of a dragon," then you must be resolute about your practice and try seriously to bring it into every aspect of your life.

✌ Exchanging Chi with a Partner

Here's another chi exchange exercise you can do with your partner. This one is a bit advanced, so it might be better to practice it after each of you has established your own chi gong practice. It uses the Small Orbit, an ancient form of chi gong cultivation.

One partner should sit in the lap of the other, your arms around each other. If practicing with a partner of the opposite sex, the male's lingam can be inserted into the woman's yoni. You can either stay still or move just enough to maintain an erection.

Then, either with eyes closed or looking into each other's eyes, begin the basic chi gong breath. Each of you breathe into your lower abdomen until you feel some heat or movement there or until both of you are ready to move some energy.

Begin with the male or yang partner allowing his chi to sink down from his dan tian, move underneath his pelvis, and then travel back up his spine over to the top of his head. From there, it comes down the front of his body, back to his lower dan tian or his sexual organ, and then into his partner's body.

Then the woman or yin partner draws in the yang partner's chi through her yoni, or into her lower dan tian if they are not coupled, and combines it with her own. She draws it gently up her spine, over the top of her head, and then back down the front of her body to her lower dan tian or her yoni.

Then the yang partner draws her chi into his abdomen, combines it with his, and draws it gently up his spine and then back down the front of his body again.

You can spend some time exchanging and guiding chi in this way. The most important thing is not to try and force anything; just use your breath and mind to guide the energy in its pathway.

The best way to prove the efficacy of chi gong is to simply try it yourself. Its effects will be experienced in your own being. This is much better than taking the word of an author or even teacher. Try it yourself and see what it does to your own energy. As you move deeper into your own personal practice, you will be more and more able to track the changes in your life that chi gong can produce—including how it changes your love life and relationships.

essence chi gong

It is time to change the concept of searching outside the self. You must go within and find your lost genuine nature. This is the only way to free yourself. When you find your own genuine nature within, you will merge very naturally with source.

CHEN FU YIN

ESSENCE CHI GONG is a wonderful, simple, and powerful chi gong form created by a contemporary chi gong master from Beijing, Chen Fu Yin. I studied this form with him on my first trip to China in 1993 and subsequently was involved in bringing him to my town of Eugene, Oregon, to teach when he visited the United States a few years later. It was at this time that I trained with him to become an instructor. The Chinese name for this form is *Tian Di Tong Guan Gong*, or Heaven-Earth Connected Chi Gong. It is easy to learn and simple to practice, and it can help give you internal strength, stamina, and balanced internal organs. By doing this practice, both on our own and with our partner, we can bring ourselves into greater harmony, both within and without. This cannot help but have a positive and healing impact on our relationships.

Benefits and Tips

In this chi gong practice, we are doing a kind of brushing and cleansing of our energy body, first down the front and up the back, then down the back and up the front, and lastly, down the outer sides of our body and then up the inside. We do a chi massage of the five major organs of our body—our liver, heart, spleen, lungs, and kidneys. Then we hold and stimulate six important energetic points on our body.

After doing the movement, we stand in a meditation posture, sometimes called the Tree Pose. If we have the time to stand in this way for a while, we can experience what is called spontaneous chi gong. This is when, instead of us guiding the chi, the chi moves in its own way. The chi's movements can be gentle or quite vigorous. Sometimes the movement is accompanied by an emotional release, manifesting in crying, shouting, or even laughing. All of this is normal and can be quite healing, though it is important not to overdo this release or become so lost in a cathartic state that you lose your center. Usually you can come out of it very easily by just creating the intention to slow down and come back to your center. If you find that coming back to center is a problem, then it would probably be best to skip this part of the practice until you can obtain guidance from a qualified chi gong instructor.

The practice consists of four parts, or four routines. All four should be done in one session and in order.

The practice opens with a mantra, in which we express our intention to heal and become balanced and harmonious within and with those around us, including our partner. We make a commitment to healing and to being self-conscious, in the best sense of the word. It is in the attainment of these states that we will come into alignment with our own essential nature and of the greater nature without. We stand, a channel between heaven and earth, and run healing energy between them through our own body and being.

In the directions that follow, I have listed the lines of the mantra in both Chinese and English. I usually recommend that you recite them both ways. Some students have asked Professor Chen why we recite them in Chinese if that is not our language. He usually answered that the original words, the language in which they were first written, have a vibrational, almost magical effect. Anyone who has experienced chanting Hindu mantras will know what I mean. Most traditional Hindu mantras are written and chanted in Sanskrit, one of the most ancient languages in the world. It is believed that the actual *sounds* of the words contain special meanings, besides the literal meanings of the words themselves. For the mantra in essence chi gong, the same is true. So try reciting or chanting these beautiful Chinese words. Don't worry if you feel you are not pronouncing them correctly. Just try to *feel* what the words are saying. Then recite them in English for another level of understanding them.

A great aspect of this particular chi gong form is that it takes almost no space, uses no equipment, and benefits the whole body. It is a very internal form, done with eyes closed and in a deeply meditative state. Other chi gong forms may involve a lot of moving around, either in a circle or back and forth across the room, but in this form we stand in one place for the whole time.

The main point to remember is do each movement slowly and harmoniously, with no tension and no stress. By keeping our mind peaceful and calm, we can allow the movement of chi in our body to remove blockages and strengthen our own energetic and emotional body. By closing our eyes during the form, we are better able to concentrate on what is happening *within* us rather than without; in other words, we are better able to turn the light of our awareness inward, allowing the flower of our own heart to open and spiritual insight to blossom. In so doing, we allow for this open space to become filled with the spirit and knowledge of Tao.

Above all, this practice should be extremely enjoyable to do. If we do our practice in a tight or stressful way, the fruit of our practice will be too tight and actually unhealthy. If you feel you need to do your practice, but you are in a hurry or are in an extreme emotional state of some kind, better wait until you have more time or have calmed down. Try to do some quiet sitting or else take a walk or a bike ride or dance wildly about the house—something to change your emotional state so the fruit of your practice will be sweet and delicious. If you are exhausted, you can take a rest or a nap, though sometimes you may want to try doing the form and see if it energizes you, which sometimes happens.

A Taoist lifestyle is one of balance and harmony. It is not one of excessive demands on ourselves or others. Neither is it one of exhausting ourselves to prove something to someone else or even to ourselves. If your practice is done in a tense or extreme fashion, it may actually be harmful.

So relax and enjoy yourself! Play around with doing the practice to different types of music or nature sounds. Try doing it inside and outside your house. Practice in nature, one of the best places to do chi gong. It is believed by Taoists that it is especially good to do chi gong or meditation in the mountains. There is even a special type of energy to be found there, called *te* in Chinese. It is for this reason that many Taoist teachers and practitioners have gone to the mountains to practice and is why there are still so many Taoist centers in the mountains of China, such as in Hua Shan, Wudang and Chingcheng Shan.

Opening

Stand with your feet parallel, spaced as wide as your shoulders. Your body is straight but relaxed. The bai hui (crown chakra) is pointing upward.

Tuck your chin slightly inward so the neck is straight. Relax your jaw and close your lips; your teeth are touching lightly. Put the tip of your tongue on the upper palate of your mouth. Slowly close your eyes.

Very slowly, relax your body from top to bottom: head, neck, chest, upper back, shoulders, upper arms, elbows, forearms, wrists, palms, fingers, belly, hips, cervical vertebrae, thoracic vertebrae, lumbar vertebrae, coccyx, groin, thighs, knees, calves, ankles, feet, toes, and mind.

Next, it is very important to do the rooting exercise presented in chapter 11. Send roots down from the bottoms of your feet, deep into the earth, at least five times the length of your body. This can enhance your experience immeasurably. As a matter of fact, you should do this any time you practice chi gong or tai chi. Grounding and rooting yourself in the earth will give you much more power than if you just start your form without rooting.

Don't worry about having to go through the floor or even through several floors if you are on the second or third floor of a building. The energy will go through these barriers easily. It is the strength of your mind that makes this happen. This rooting practice in itself is a very powerful training and will enhance whatever kind of energetic or spiritual practice you engage in.

Now say these universal sounds, the mantra of intention, aloud three times:

Ding tian li di
Standing with head in heaven and feet on earth,
Song jing zi ran
Relaxed and natural.
Ren he yu zhou
In harmony with the universe,
Tian di tong guan
I am a channel between heaven and earth.

Routine One: Unity of Heaven and Earth

Lift your arms up to shoulder height, palms down, with wrists relaxed. Then allow your arms to float down to your lower dan tian. Repeat three to nine times. This will help charge up your palms, or lao gong points, with chi.

Routine Two: Movement between Heaven and Earth

Part One: After the last repetition of routine one, when your hands are at the lower dan tian, turn your palms to face one another and raise your extended arms up until they are over the bai hui. Stop for a moment here and beam healing chi from your lao gong points in your palms into your bai hui point.

Push your elbows a bit outward and to the sides as you relax your wrists over your head.

With your palms facing your body, move your arms downward, the slower the better. As your palms move past your face, trunk, and legs, they comb through your energy body.

When your hands reach your thighs, let your palms continue down over the front of your thighs and then your legs as you slowly bow down from the waist. Your hands move over the tops of your feet, then around the sides of your feet to your ankles, and then to the backs of your heels. Begin to move your palms up along the back of your legs, straightening your body, vertebra by vertebra, while your hands move up to your lower back.

Your elbows are out to the sides as you draw your hands forward along the belt channel (around the waist) and to the front of your body, in front of your navel. Hold them there, one on top of the other, for a moment in front of your lower dan tian, breathing gently into this area. (Men, put your right hand over your left. Women, put your left hand over your right.)

Repeat the entire part-one sequence three to nine times.

Part Two: This time bring your arms straight out from your sides, palms facing up. Your arms are extended out from your shoulders ninety degrees, so your body is the shape of a letter "t." Lift your arms up over your head, bring your hands close together, palms facing down, wrists relaxed. Beam chi from lao gong points in your palms into the bai hui point.

Move your hands downward behind your head and stretch them downward as far as you can, palms facing the back of your head and neck. (You will only be able to reach to the bottom of your neck.)

Pull your hands forward over your trapezius muscles (the muscles connecting your neck and shoulders) to the front of your shoulders, then move your hands under your armpits to your upper back.

Turn palms to face your back and move downward along the mid back, the lower back, buttocks, and legs, all the way to the heels. Your palms are not actually touching your body, but are combing through your chi body, which extends several inches outside of your body.

Move your palms around the sides of your feet to the toes. Then bring your palms upward along the front of your legs, up to your waist, straightening your body vertebra by vertebra until you are standing completely upright.

Bring your hands over your dan tian again and breathe into this area, same as in part one.

Repeat the entire part-two sequence three to nine times.

Part Three: After the last repetition of part two, your hands are on your lower dan tian. Separate them and extend them out in front of your body at a forty-five-degree angle, palm facing palm.

Lift your arms upward until your hands are above your head. Relax your wrists over your bai hui, beaming heavenly chi into this area.

Bend your arms and move your palms downward along the sides of your face. Again, your palms are not touching your physical body, but are several inches away from it, moving through your chi body.

With the palms still facing your body, turn your fingers downward and keep moving your hands along the sides of your body as you bow forward. Keep moving your hands along the outsides of your thighs, knees, lower legs, and ankles. Keep moving your hands along the sides of your feet to the toes.

Turn your hands to face the inner edges of your feet. Move them upward, along the inner sides of your ankles, lower legs, and thighs, as you straighten your body. When your hands reach your groin, continue moving them over the front of your abdomen until your hands reach your navel.

Bring your hands over your dan tian again and breathe into this area, same as in parts one and two.

Repeat the entire part-three sequence three to nine times.

Routine Three: Rotating Chi around Five Internal Organs

Once your hands are in front of your lower dan tian, guide them to the liver, located under the right side of the rib cage. Hold your hands a few inches away from your body, over your liver area, and let there be space between your two hands. Make nine clockwise circles over this area. You can visualize the color green here and picture your liver as healthy and vibrant.

Slowly move your hands to the heart center, again keeping your hands a few inches away from the physical body. Make nine clockwise circles over this area. Here you can visualize the color red and your heart center as healthy and vibrant.

Slowly move your hands to your spleen area, located under the left side of the rib cage. Holding your hands apart and a few inches away from the physical body, make nine clockwise circles over this area. Here you can visualize the color yellow and your spleen, as well as your stomach, as healthy and vibrant.

Now pull your hands up over the lungs, in the upper chest. Both hands meet in the middle of the collarbone and then move down the middle of the chest along the inner edges of the left and right lung, then circle up the outside. Here you can visualize the color white and see your lungs as healthy and vibrant. Repeat this circular pattern over the lungs nine times.

After the last repetition, move your hands around your waist to your lower back, palms facing the kidneys. Move your hands together up the center of your lower back and then separate them. The left hand moves outward to the left, circling down and around the outside of the left kidney area; the right hand does the same on the other side. Here you can visualize the color black and your kidneys and adrenals as being vibrant and healthy. Repeat the circular movement nine times.

Routine Four: Going through the Three Dan Tians

Extend your arms out behind you, palm facing palm. Draw your arms forward, keeping them extended as you do.

Bring your arms upward, bending your elbows slightly, so your hands are at the level of your head. The palms are toward your face, and your fingers are slightly bent, so the fingertips are also pointing toward your face.

Draw the tips of your middle fingers together and press them lightly to the point between your eyes (the tian mu or third eye point). Beam chi into this point through your fingertips as they gently press into this point. Hold this position for three to nine deep breaths. (After you have practiced this form for a while, you will begin to feel the chi gently pushing your fingers away from the tian mu point.)

Lower your fingertips to the shan zhong or heart center point, in the middle of the chest between the breasts. This is also known as the middle dan tian. As before, your middle fingers come together and touch this point. With your fingertips, beam chi into this point. Hold this position for three to nine deep breaths.

Lower your fingertips to what is known as the zhong wan point, halfway between the breastbone and the navel. Your middle fingers should come together and touch this point. With your fingertips, beam chi into this point. Hold this position for three to nine deep breaths.

Move your fingertips down to your navel. Touch this point with the tips of your middle fingers and beam chi into this point. Hold this position for three to nine deep breaths.

Lower your hands and place your palms over your lower dan tian—right hand over left for men, and left hand over right for women. Beam chi into this place through your palms. Hold this position for three to nine deep breaths.

Separate your hands and move them around your waist to your lower back. Place your palms on the middle of your back, one over the other, between your kidneys, a point known as the *ming men*. Beam chi into this place through your palms. Hold this position for three to nine deep breaths.

Ending: Coming Back to Your True Nature

When you finish with routine four, bring your palms back to your lower dan tian. Stand and breath deeply, with eyes closed, for at least nine deep, slow breaths, sealing healing chi into your lower dan tian. Feel the chi moving in all your channels and organs in a smooth and balanced way. When you feel ready, slowly open your eyes.

conclusion

I WANT TO thank you, my readers, for coming on this journey with me. For those of you who have been moved to explore a little more of the world of Taoism, great. For those of you who are more interested in the concepts and practices of this book without feeling the need to know more about Taoism, also great. I am not looking for converts; I simply wish to share what I have learned in my studies of Taoist philosophy and practice, as well as the always interesting world of relationship.

I was married for twenty-five years to a remarkable woman who shared the same birthday with me. We raised three amazing children and went on many life journeys together. At the end of twenty-five years, we went our separate ways, and it was nine months (a time of great gestation) later that I met my current partner, Shanti (whose birthday is the day before mine).

A beautiful woman, Shanti had a lot of relationship issues and had never lived with a man before we met. We had a lot to work through. But it was very exciting and gratifying to discover that my Taoist training was of great use in working through our issues. The Taoist principles of going slowly, being in the moment, accepting another person completely for who they are in any given moment, not forcing (wu wei), being okay with what was happening rather than what I wished was happening, being emotionally flexible, going with the flow in each moment, and being a "deep listener" were all of great help as we got to know each other.

I was in my mid-fifties when Shanti and I got together. Beginning a new relationship in my "middle age" was very different than starting one in my late twenties. (This is why I call Shanti "the great love of my middle years.") I was able to be much more conscious about my choices than I was when in my youth. Moving slowly and letting the relationship develop naturally was much easier.

Yet spiritual maturity can come at any time. All spiritual teachings are concerned with union with the divine, or Source, what the Chinese call Tao. Ultimately it is through our deep connection with Source that we create and sustain a deep connection with someone else. It is in our self-cultivation of our own mature spiritual being that we will be able to achieve sacred union, with all its intimacy and ecstasy, with another person.

Taoists see all the various aspects of practice as one practice. The sexual practices, the tai chi of communion, the opening and healing of the heart, the deep meditation practice, the health-enhancing practice of chi gong, learning and dancing the Watercourse Way, even the energetics of emotions—they are really all aspects of one practice: the practice of being a self-realized or an authentic human being, what the Taoists call zhen ren.

Lao Tzu describes these people like this:

> To know others is wisdom
> but to know one's self is enlightenment.
> Those who conquer others
> require great power.
> But to conquer one's self
> requires inner strength.
> Those who know they have enough
> are wealthy.
> Those who persevere have strong will.
> Those who are not separated
> from their center
> will long endure.
> (Chapter 10)

In this age of overstimulation and instant communication, there is still a great need for balanced, harmonious, and grounded relationship practices and attitudes. Taoists are very practical and down to earth. It is my hope that the Taoist principles explored in this book will help you create, develop, and sustain sacred union. If you find something that works for you, by all means pursue it. If, on the other hand, some of the practices and principles in this book are not relevant to you, forget them and move on. Ultimately, it is up to each of us to forge relationships that serve us emotionally, physically, and spiritually. It is indeed a lofty goal, but that is the relationship that each of us deserves!

works cited

Chia, Mantak, and Michael Winn. *Taoist Secrets of Love: Cultivating Male Sexual Energy.* Santa Fe, NM: Aurora Press, 1984.

Huang, Chungliang Al. *Tai Ji.* Berkeley, CA: Celestial Arts, 1989.

Ni, Hua Ching. *8,000 Years of Wisdom.* Malibu, CA: SevenStar Communications, 1983.

_____. *The Gentle Path of Spiritual Progress.* Malibu, CA: SevenStar Communications, 1987.

_____. *Harmony, The Art of Life.* Malibu, CA: SevenStar Communications, 1991.

_____. *Moonlight in the Dark Night.* Malibu, CA: SevenStar Communications, 1991.

Reid, Daniel. *The Tao of Health, Sex, and Longevity.* New York: Simon and Schuster, 1989.

Towler, Solala. *Tales from the Tao.* London: Watkins, 2005.

_____. *The Inner Chapters of Chuang Tzu.* London: Watkins Publishing, 2010.

Tzu, Lao. *Tao Te Ching.* Translated by Solala Towler. Unpublished manuscript.

resources

Taoism

Blofeld, John. *Taoism: The Road to Immortality.* Shambhala, 1985.

Mair, Victor H. *Wandering on the Way.* Bantam Books, 1994.

Miller, James. *Daoism: A Short Introduction.* Oneworld Publications, 2003.

Ming Dao, Deng. *Chronicles of Tao.* HarperSanFransisco, 1993.

_____. *Scholar Warrior.* HarperSanFransisco, 1990.

Ni, Hua Ching. *Ageless Counsel for Modern Life.* SevenStar Publications, 1991.

Towler, Solala. *Cha Dao: The Way of Tea.* Singing Dragon, 2010.

_____. *A Gathering of Cranes: Bringing the Tao to the West.* Abode of the Eternal Tao, 1996.

_____. *Inner Chapters of Chuang Tzu.* Watkins, 2010.

_____. *Tales from the Tao.* Watkins, 2005.

Watts, Alan. *Tao: The Watercourse Way.* Random House, 1975.

Qigong

Cohen, Kenneth. *The Way of Qigong.* Ballantine Books, 1997.

Hon, Sat Chuen. *Taoist Qigong for Health and Vitality.* Shambhala, 2003.

Jahnke, Roger, *The Healer Within.* HarperCollins, 1998.

_____. *The Healing Promise of Qi.* McGraw-Hill, 2002.

Kohn, Livia. *A Source Book in Chinese Longevity.* Three Pines Press, 2012.

Leirer, Richard. *From Wu Chi to Tai Chi.* Qigong Academy Press, 2012.

Mitchell, Damo. *Heavenly Streams.* Singing Dragon, 2013.

Ni, Maoshing. *Secrets of Self-Healing.* Penguin, 2008.

Wu, Zhongxian. *Chinese Shamanic Cosmic Orbit Qigong.* Singing Dragon, 2011.

_____. *Fire Dragon Meridian Qigong.* Singing Dragon, 2012.

Yang, Jwing-Ming. *Tai Chi Qigong.* YMAA Publication Center, 2013.

Taoist Sexual Yoga

Chang, Jolan. *The Tao of Love and Sex.* E.P. Dutton, 1977.

Chang, Stephen T. *The Tao of Sexology.* Tao Publishing, 1986.

Chia, Mantak, and Kris Deva North. *Taoist Foreplay.* Destiny Books, 2005.

Chian, Zettnersan. *Taoist Bedroom Secrets.* Lotus Press, 2002.

Chu, Valentin. *The Yin-Yang Butterfly.* Jeremy P. Tarcher, 1993.

Frantzis, Bruce. *Taoist Sexual Meditation.* Energy Arts, 2012.

Heng, Cheng. *The Tao of Love.* Marlowe and Co., 1997.

Lai, Hsi. *The Sexual Teachings of the White Tigress: Secrets of the Female Taoist Masters.* Destiny Books, 2001.

_____. *The Sexual Teachings of the Jade Dragon: Taoist Methods for Male Sexual Revitalization.* Destiny Books, 2002.

Villecroix, Serge. *Sex Mudras.* Destiny Books, 2013.

Wile, Douglas. *Art of the Bedchamber: The Chinese Sexual Yoga Classics Including Women's Solo Meditation Texts.* State University of New York Press, 1992.

Websites

Abode of the Eternal Tao (Solala Towler)
Empty Vessel: The Journal of Daoist Philosophy and Practice
abodetao.com

Dao of Well Being (Rebecca Kali)
dao-of-well-being.com

Energy Arts (Bruce Frantzis)
energyarts.com

Healing Tao USA (Michael Winn)
healingtaousa.com

Institute of Integral Qigong and Tai Chi (Roger Jahnke)
instituteofintegralqigongandtaichi.org

National Qigong Association
nqa.org

Qigong Academy (Richard Leirer)
richardleirer.org

Three Pines Press (Livia Kohn)
threepinespress.com

Yang-Sheng Magazine
yang-sheng.com

acknowledgments

GRATEFUL THANKS TO Jennifer Brown for welcoming me to the Sounds True family and to Amy Rost for wrestling the manuscript into much better shape than I could by myself. And to all of my teachers—past, present, and future.

about the author

SOLALA TOWLER has taught and practiced Taoist meditation and chi gong (qigong) for more than twenty-five years. He is the author of fourteen books, including *Tales from the Tao* and *Tao Paths to Love*. Since 1993, he has edited and published *The Empty Vessel: The Journal of Daoist Philosophy and Practice*, which is available in print and online. He teaches chi gong and sound healing at conferences and workshops throughout the United States and abroad and is a founding board member and past president of the National Qigong Association. He leads tours to China to visit the sacred mountains and temples of Taoism. In addition, he is founder of the sacred music ensemble Windhorse and has recorded four CDs of music for chi gong, tai chi, meditation, or yoga. He lives in Eugene, Oregon. For more information on his chi gong training or his tours to China, please visit abodetao.com.

about sounds true

SOUNDS TRUE is a multimedia publisher whose mission is to inspire and support personal transformation and spiritual awakening. Founded in 1985 and located in Boulder, Colorado, we work with many of the leading spiritual teachers, thinkers, healers, and visionary artists of our time. We strive with every title to preserve the essential "living wisdom" of the author or artist. It is our goal to create products that not only provide information to a reader or listener, but that also embody the quality of a wisdom transmission.

For those seeking genuine transformation, Sounds True is your trusted partner. At SoundsTrue.com you will find a wealth of free resources to support your journey, including exclusive weekly audio interviews, free downloads, interactive learning tools, and other special savings on all our titles.

To learn more, please visit SoundsTrue.com/bonus/free_gifts or call us toll free at 800-333-9185.

sounds true
many voices, one journey